The Inuit

The Inuit

Titles in the Indigenous Peoples of North America series Include:

The Inuit

Anne Wallace Sharp

Lucent Books, Inc.

10911 Technology Place, San Diego, California 92127

Library of Congress Cataloging-in-Publication Data

Sharp, Anne Wallace
    The Inuit / by Anne Wallace Sharp.
        p.   cm. — (Indigenous peoples of North America)
Includes bibliographical references and index.
Summary: Presents a history of native American people of the Arctic,
describes their adaptation to a severe environment, and explores their way
of life before and after the arrival of the white man.
    ISBN 1-59018-006-2 (alk. paper)
    1. Inuit—Juvenile literature. [1. Inuit. 2. Eskimos.] I. Title. II. Series.
E99.E7 S457 2002
971.9'0049712—dc21

2001004227

© 2002 Lucent Books
an imprint of The Gale Group
10911 Technology Place, San Diego, California 92127

Printed in the U.S.A.

Contents

Foreword

North America's native peoples are often relegated to history—viewed primarily as remnants of another era—or cast in the stereotypical images long found in popular entertainment and even literature. Efforts to characterize Native Americans typically result in idealized portrayals of spiritualists communing with nature or bigoted descriptions of savages incapable of living in civilized society. Lost in these unfortunate images is the rich variety of customs, beliefs, and values that comprised—and still comprise—many of North America's native populations.

The *Indigenous Peoples of North America* series strives to present a complex, realistic picture of the many and varied Native American cultures. Each book in the series offers historical perspectives as well as a view of contemporary life of individual tribes and tribes that share a common region. The series examines traditional family life, spirituality, interaction with other native and non-native peoples, warfare, and the ways the environment shaped the lives and cultures of North America's indigenous populations. Each book ends with a discussion of life today for the Native Americans of a given region or tribe.

In any discussion of the Native American experience, there are bound to be sim-ilarities. All tribes share a past filled with unceasing white expansion and resistance that led to more than four hundred years of conflict. One U.S. administration after another pursued this goal and fought Indians who attempted to defend their homelands and ways of life. Although no war was ever formally declared, the U.S. policy of conquest precluded any chance of white and Native American peoples living together peacefully. Between 1780 and 1890, Americans killed hundreds of thousands of Indians and wiped out whole tribes.

The Indians lost the fight for their land and ways of life, though not for lack of bravery, skill, or a sense of purpose. They simply could not contend with the overwhelming numbers of whites arriving from Europe or the superior weapons they brought with them. Lack of unity also contributed to the defeat of the Native Americans. For most, tribal identity was more important than racial identity. This loyalty left the Indians at a distinct disadvantage. Whites had a strong racial identity and they fought alongside each other even when there was disagreement, because they shared a racial destiny.

Although all Native Americans share this tragic history they have many distinct differences. For example, some tribes and individuals sought to cooperate almost immediately with the U.S. government while others steadfastly resisted the white presence. Life before the arrival of white settlers also varied. The nomads of the Plains developed altogether different lifestyles and customs from the fishermen of the Northwest coast.

Contemporary life is no different in this regard. Many Native Americans—forced onto reservations by the American government—struggle with poverty, poor health, and inferior schooling. But others have regained a sense of pride in themselves and their heritage, enabling them to search out new routes to self-sufficiency and prosperity.

The *Indigenous Peoples of North America* series attempts to capture the differences as well as similarities that make up the experiences of North America's native populations—both past and present. Fully documented primary and secondary source quotations enliven the text. Sidebars highlight events, personalities, and traditions. Bibliographies provide readers with ideas for further research. In all, each book in this dynamic series provides students with a wealth of information as well as launching points for further research.

Who Are the Inuit?

Toward the end of the last ice age around twelve thousand years ago, a land bridge connected northeastern Asia to the present-day state of Alaska. Thousands of people—the first immigrants to the New World—crossed over this bridge in search of food and new land. In the years that followed, their descendants spread south into the continents of North and South America. These individuals settled all over the Americas and formed the various native groups who would, years later, be called Indians.

Nearly nine thousand years later, around 3000 B.C., the last group of people arrived from Asia. By this time the land bridge had long since vanished. These hardy individuals made the crossing over the icy seas of the Bering Strait between Siberia and Alaska in skin-covered boats. Rather than heading south after their arrival, like so many others before them, this group stayed in northern Alaska in an area of the world called the Arctic. These people were the ancestors of today's Inuit.

From the beginning of their history, the Inuit followed a nomadic hunting and fishing lifestyle as they moved from one location to another in search of food. Remarkably, they were also able to adapt to the intensely cold climate of the Arctic in a number of unique

A miniature mask, dating from 500 B.C., was probably used as a shaman's device.

ways—all without the aid of modern technology. Over a period of four thousand years they gradually moved over the vast Arctic, from the eastern tip of Siberia, across Alaska and northern Canada, to Greenland—a distance of more than three thousand miles. That these prehistoric people were able to survive and establish a permanent homeland in the Arctic is, according to Philip Kopper, "a human miracle of the first magnitude."[1]

Early Inuit Society

The first distinctive Inuit society was known as the Arctic Small Tool Culture. These people hunted sea mammals such as whales, walruses, and seals. They made simple tools and left behind many small carvings of animals. They eventually moved overland from Alaska into the western part of Canada.

Beginning around 1000 B.C., the Small Tool Culture was gradually replaced by what archaeologists refer to as the Dorset Culture. These people built snow houses and invented a unique kind of boat called the kayak that greatly increased their success at hunting.

Eventually the Dorset Culture gave way to the Thule Culture around A.D. 1000. This group was the first to use dogsleds as they continued their settlement of the Arctic. They moved east, through Canada, until they ultimately reached Greenland, a large island in the North Atlantic. Choosing not to move south because of hostile neighbors, the Thule people referred to themselves as the *Sivullirimiut,* or "first ones."

Historians have never been able to state with any assurance how many Inuit lived in North America prior to the coming of the

A comb, dating from A.D. 1000, features the shape of a stylized female figure.

white man. It has been difficult to make an estimate because of the large number of small villages and vast territory of the Arctic. Most scholars place the number of Inuit somewhere between fifty thousand and one hundred thousand.

Isolated at the top of the world in a land of bitter cold, wild storms, and winter darkness, the Inuit evolved into one of the world's most distinctive cultures. Various Indian groups to the south called their Arctic neighbors Eskimo, which meant "eaters of raw flesh." The

Inuit, to whom the term was applied, found it insulting. They preferred to be called Inuit, meaning simply "the people." (The word *Inuk* means one person.) The word *Eskimo* does not even exist in the Inuit language.

Each group of Inuit had its own customs and rules of conduct. Each community also developed its own lifestyle based on the animals available for hunting in its area. Despite these differences, Inuit life was remarkably similar wherever their location.

One Inuit leader writes: "As Inuit we divide ourselves into two closely related groups: the Yupik of southwest Alaska and Russia, and the Inupiat of northern Alaska, Canada and Greenland. One of the truly amazing aspects of our culture is the extent of similarity from one group to another as you travel across three thousand miles."[2]

An Epic Tale

Significant change for the Inuit did not occur until well into the nineteenth century. Because of their isolation, the Inuit were among the last native peoples in the New World to be affected by the coming of the white man. The Inuit, unlike other Native Americans, never went to war with the white man. However, as early as the sixteenth century, explorers, fur traders, whalers, and missionaries moved into their homelands and began to affect Inuit society. The result was a growing dependence on white society and the goods it produced.

These changes accelerated in the twentieth century as the Inuit were forced to move from their native hunting grounds. They were not placed on reservations but rather taken from

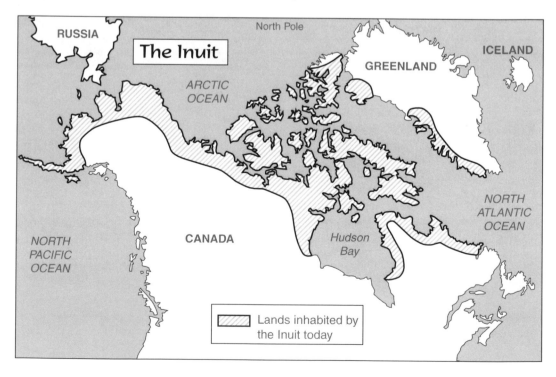

their traditional homelands and relocated to permanent villages and towns. These moves caused additional changes in Inuit society, and many of the old ways of life suffered.

Today, the Inuit, like other Native American groups, struggle with such modern problems as poverty, unemployment, and alcoholism. In spite of these concerns, the Inuit are optimistic as they move into the twenty-first century. Many Inuit have gained independence through native land settlement agreements in both Canada and Alaska. Inuit leaders continue to be instrumental as they work to gain recognition for the Inuit as a distinct people.

The Inuit today have the most widespread population in the world. Their people are spread across four countries with around 47,000 Inuit living in Greenland, 44,000 in Alaska, 35,000 in Canada, and 1,700 in Siberia. Despite the great distances between settlements and groups of Inuit, there is a remarkable degree of unity that still ties these groups together today.

Over the last fifty years the Inuit have worked tirelessly to preserve their history and traditions. According to one *Inuk*, "Our history is an epic tale in the history of human settlement and the endurance of our culture. Our history is about people and their relationship to the environment and to each other; about dealing with change; and . . . about how we as a culture were able to live in balance with the natural world."[3]

Chapter 1

Surviving in a Harsh Land

The Inuit are the original inhabitants of the Arctic and are, in many ways, one of the most remarkable of all the native peoples of North America. They live in one of the harshest natural environments on the face of the earth. These lands are described by Canadian archaeologist Robert McGee as the "coldest, darkest and most barren regions ever inhabited by man."[4]

No one is really sure why the Inuit chose to settle in the Arctic. One reason may be that the climate was actually warmer there than in Siberia, where they had come from. Or perhaps they found the hunting so good that they decided to stay. Another possible reason is that the Inuit, a peaceful people for the most part, did not wish to challenge their more warlike neighbors to the south. For whatever reason, the Inuit chose to stay in the Arctic. There, with incredible imagination and determination, they created a way of life amidst the snow, wind, and ice.

Instead of trying to fight and conquer the difficult environment, the Inuit learned instead to use it to their advantage. Every aspect of their lives began in some kind of response to the harsh conditions under which they lived. The Inuit learned how to find animals in the snowy landscape. They learned how to figure out the wind direction and how to predict the movement of the ice. They learned how to navigate the seas during thick fog and dark nights simply by the feel of the ocean currents. And they learned to travel on fast dogsleds and developed the world's most efficient cold weather clothing and housing. "Of all the peoples in the history of the world, they were among the toughest, most resourceful and most adaptable,"[5] writes historian Paula Younkin.

Arctic Weather

The Inuit call their Arctic homeland *Nunatsiaq*—the beautiful land. The Arctic includes the Arctic Ocean, thousands of islands, and the northernmost parts of the continents of Europe, Asia, and North America. It also includes all of Greenland and most of Iceland.

Viewed from space, the Arctic is clearly visible as a patch of white sitting on top of our planet. It looks white because it is covered most of the year by ice and snow. The Arctic is also one of the coldest places on earth. The main reason the Arctic is so cold is that the ice cap at the North Pole acts like a giant mirror and instead of absorbing the sun's heat, reflects much of it back into space. Another reason for the cold is that the farther north one travels, the less heat the sun actually provides. Nearer the equator, the sun appears more directly overhead and the heat is thus more intense. But in the Arctic, the sun never rises very high above the horizon.

As a result, temperatures in the Arctic during the winter average between twenty and thirty degrees below zero Fahrenheit, but can be as low as ninety to one hundred below in some areas. Even during the summer the temperature seldom rises much above fifty. The snow and ice around the Arctic Circle and North Pole never melt, even in the summertime.

Fierce winds blow across the Arctic most of the year. During the winter, the winds are

Arctic hares rest on the Canadian tundra, an area where the snow never melts.

nearly intolerable, dropping temperatures even lower because of windchill. Coming from every direction, the winds cause nearly constant swirling masses of blowing snow and can whip up a blizzard very quickly. Very few living things can survive in the Arctic without protection from these strong winds. Arctic animals had to develop thick layers of fur and fat, while plants were forced to hug the ground to survive.

The longest season in the Arctic is the winter, which can last up to nine months. It is so cold during this time that people's and animals' breath can actually steam and freeze in midair. Beginning in late September or October, winter descends on the Arctic and the sun appears above the horizon for less time each passing day. By December 21, the winter solstice, there is no daylight at all. This period of time is often referred to as the polar night.

By the middle of May the sun begins to appear above the horizon for a longer period of time each day, but it is still too cold for the snow to melt. Summer lasts only eight weeks, and at its height the sun never sets.

The Origin of Wind

The Inuit, like native peoples everywhere, use stories and myths to explain the mysteries of the world around them. These tales are passed down from generation to generation by word of mouth. They are still told to Inuit children today. The following story explains why the Arctic is so windy. The tale is retold by Lawrence Millman in his book *A Kayak Full of Ghosts: Eskimo Tales.* It is presented here in a condensed form.

Long ago, there was a huge ice bear who carried a sack in which he kept all the wind in the world. He would not permit anyone to open this sack. There lived also a hunter, and he was very curious about what was inside the bear's sack.

"What's in your sack?" he asked.

"Just a big load of poop, that's all," the bear replied.

"But why are you carrying it around?"

"Who knows?" said the bear. "I might get hungry while I'm traveling over the ice."

The hunter thought this was crazy and did not believe the bear for a minute. He wanted very badly to see what was in the sack so he sang the bear to sleep. When the bear finally dozed off, the hunter opened the sack. Out came the wind.

It knocked the hunter down and then sped away in every direction.

The hunter was very alarmed. "Oh, Great Bear," he cried. "You can have my wife for a month if you'll only get rid of this horrible wind."

But the bear only shook his head. Wind had just entered the world.

Thick layers of fur and fat help reindeer survive the harsh temperatures of the Arctic.

This phenomenon is known as the midnight sun and occurs from the middle of June to the beginning of August.

The Tundra

Most Inuit occupy a part of the Arctic called the tundra. The tundra is a harsh, treeless land that lies between the great pine forests of northern North America and the Arctic Circle. During the winter, the lakes and rivers there freeze over and the land is covered with snow. During the summer, low-lying areas become wet and marshy.

The primary characteristic of the tundra is the lack of trees. Trees simply cannot grow where the temperature is so cold. Nor can they stand up to the fierce winter winds that blow constantly. The low temperatures, strong winds, poor soil, and short summers make life very hard for all but the hardiest of plants. Only those plants that are low to the ground survive. Tundra vegetation forms a low, continuous mat only a few inches high. This mat is generally made up of moss, which is a small, leafy growth along the ground, and sedge, a grasslike plant that grows only where it is wet.

The Arctic tundra is extremely fragile and when damaged takes much longer to heal than anywhere else in the world. Tire tracks,

Foxes are one of several varieties of animals that make the Arctic their home.

for instance, stay there for over fifty years. Garbage takes about the same number of years to decay because bacteria, which is necessary to break down the waste, cannot live in the frigid temperatures.

The Arctic is a place where it seems impossible that there would be any life at all. In spite of appearances, however, the region is home to a wide variety of life, including the Inuit. Wolves, foxes, caribou, and polar bears all make their home in the Arctic. The sea also provides its share of wildlife in the form of seals, walruses, whales, and fish. Each of these animals has adapted to life in the Arctic by growing thick fur or layers of fat called blubber. In addition, thousands of birds come to the Arctic to take advantage of the rich vegetation, plentiful insects, and space for nesting.

Staying Warm

When the Inuit began to spread across the Arctic from Alaska to Greenland, they faced the supreme challenge of trying to withstand the harsh conditions. With no wood for fires and no wool to make clothes, the Inuit had to find other ways to survive. To do this, they had to find, first of all, a way to stay warm. No one could live through the icy winters without the proper clothing.

The Inuit made all of their clothes from the skins of animals. Styles varied from region to region, but everywhere men, women, and children wore the same general outfit. This consisted of a hooded jacket called a parka, trousers or leggings, socks, boots, and mittens.

The Inuit preferred the skin of the caribou (a large kind of deer found in northern climates, also known as reindeer) as material for their clothing. According to qualified observers, the caribou parka is the most effective cold weather clothing ever invented. The skins were usually easy to obtain and very effective in keeping the Inuit warm.

Caribou skin is lightweight and covered with hollow inner hairs that trap warm air inside, making a parka snug and cozy even on the coldest day. Most Inuit wore two layers of clothing during the winter—an inner suit with the fur next to the skin and an outer suit with the fur on the outside. The air between the layers provided insulation and additional warmth.

The parka fit loosely over the head, neck, and shoulders, and was usually big enough that the Inuit could pull their arms inside for extra warmth during the winter. New mothers wore special hooded coats that allowed babies to breathe while being carried on their mother's back. In warmer weather only the inner layer was worn.

The hoods of caribou-skin coats carried babies on their mothers' backs.

Arctic Clothing and Survival Gear

Clothing a family of four usually required around twenty different skins—seven for the man, six for the woman, and three to four apiece for each child. Women spent much of their days cutting and sewing the caribou skins into garments. Sitting on the floor of their dwellings, the Inuit women used a semi-circular knife called an *ulu* to scrape and cut the skins.

After cutting the skins, women chewed and rubbed the material to make it soft. Chewing was a vital part of the sewing process but it had its side effects. The teeth of many older Inuit women got worn right down to the gums from this practice. After softening the hides, the women stitched them together using a bone needle and strong thread made of animal muscle or sinew.

In addition to the parka, most Inuit wore boots, or mukluks, which were made of waterproof sealskin. This skin kept their feet

An Inuit woman softens caribou skins with her teeth before sewing them together.

dry when they were on the ice or near the water. This kind of boot was usually worn only in the summer. During the winter, Inuit boots were made of several layers of caribou skin. Dried grass was spread between the layers of skin to provide insulation for the feet.

In addition to inventing the parka, the Inuit made another important contribution to Arctic clothing. They invented sunglasses long before Europeans thought to do so. Because the reflection of the sun off the snow and ice could cause a temporary loss of vision called snow blindness, the Inuit often wore goggles made of wood, bone, or ivory. A small hole or narrow slit was cut into the bone, allowing the Inuit to see without being in danger from the glare.

The Inuit were also the first group of people in North America to use crampons. Made out of bone or ivory, these sharp points were lashed to their boot soles to make walking on the ice easier and less treacherous. These devices are used today by mountain climbers around the world.

Over the past few hundred years, Inuit clothing has changed very little. Modern clothing is now widely available in the Arctic and, in villages, most teenagers wear jeans, sneakers, and other sportswear. But not in the winter. The Inuit today still wear their parkas during the long winter months. Despite the recent addition of brightly colored Gore-Tex suits for mountain climbing, the parka remains, according to qualified scientists, one of the warmest and most durable of all Arctic garments.

Building a Snow House

Despite their warm clothing, it would have been impossible for the Inuit to survive in the Arctic without some kind of warm housing. They noticed that many Arctic animals survived by digging down into the snow to keep warm. The Inuit learned from the animals and invented special houses that would enable them to survive the frigid cold and bitter winds.

The words *Eskimo* and *Inuit* usually make people think of the igloo. Although many think that the word *igloo* means a house of snow, it does not—the word actually refers to any kind of house. The Inuit, depending on where they lived, built many different kinds of homes.

In western Alaska, for instance, most houses were built of stone or sod, whereas in the southern part of Alaska, dwellings were usually made out of wood. Only the Inuit of central Canada and the northern Arctic islands lived in snow houses all winter. Most Inuit, instead, built snow houses as temporary shelters while traveling or hunting.

A snow house, or as the Inuit say *illuviga,* was built of tightly packed snow and shaped like a dome to keep the heat inside. The entire family helped in building this home. First the husband sketched a circle in the snow anywhere from nine to fifteen feet in diameter. Standing inside this circle, the man cleared away the surface snow and then began to cut out blocks of hard-packed snow, called *igluksak*, from within the circle. He placed the first row of large blocks along the rim of his outline. Each row after that would curve upward and slightly inward until the snow house was about nine feet high.

Tents and Sod Houses

When spring came it was time for the Inuit to move into their summer tents. These structures were easy to assemble and could be moved from place to place. The tents were made of seal or walrus skins and could provide a comfortable home for an Inuit family. The tent posts were made of long animal bones or driftwood that washed up on shore when the ice started to melt. A small community of several Inuit families would share a campsite. These camps usually grew up around summer hunting sites.

Where there were nearby forests, as in southern Alaska, the Inuit usually built partially underground homes made of wood and sod. The key to comfort here was the earth itself, for it provided warmth and insulation during the cold winters. The Inuit men would dig about three feet down to fashion out a living space. Over this area they built a frame made out of whatever they could find—driftwood, whalebone, or the like. Once the frame was built, layers of sod were closely packed to form the walls and the roof. Many Alaskan Inuit occupied these houses year round—they were called *barabaras*.

The inner room of the sod house was similar to the one found in the snow house. Light entered through a hole cut in the wall that was covered with a piece of a sea mammal's intestine. Entry was again through a long tunnel. Frequently a storehouse was attached to these houses. Frozen, dried, or salted meat could be kept for months in these storage areas.

A tent framed by long animal bones and covered with seal or walrus skins provides shelter in the summer.

A snow house takes shape as blocks are cut from hard-packed snow and stacked in rows that move inward and upward.

As he worked, his wife and children covered the outside of the house with soft snow, packing it into any spaces left between the blocks. The entire outside construction generally took only a couple of hours. "To watch an Eskimo build an igloo was to see a true artisan at work,"[6] said an unidentified observer in the nineteenth century.

It takes weeks and months to build a house of wood, stone, or bricks, but the Inuit were able to accomplish this task from snow in a matter of hours. The end result was a warm home in which the Inuit could comfortably survive during the worst blizzards the Arctic could produce. Despite advances in technology, nothing that modern society can produce matches the snow house in simplicity, design, and warmth. They were—and are—true works of art.

Finishing a Snow House

Once the outside was complete, the husband usually cut a hole in the house to serve as a door. Nearly always, a tunnel from ten to twenty feet long was then built leading away from the house. The tunnel served to prevent the cold Arctic wind from blowing directly into the home. To reach the front door from the outside, family members had to crawl on their hands and knees through the tunnel.

A hole was also cut in the ceiling for ventilation. The hole was large enough to allow stagnant air to go out, but too small for cold air to enter. Another hole served as a small window. A block of clear ice or a clear piece of sealskin was used to cover the window hole. While not totally transparent, the window did allow some light to enter the house.

Sleek kayaks glide silently across the water.

Inside the snow house the Inuit built a snow ledge, or *illiq,* about two feet off the floor. This area was used for eating, sleeping, and sitting. The family usually all slept together on the snow ledge beneath blankets made of fox, caribou, or bearskin. Waterproof sealskin and other furs were used underneath them as insulation against the moisture and cold of the snow ledge.

A lamp, or *quilliq,* was used to heat the inside and for cooking. Most lamps were small and round in shape and made of hollowed-out soapstone, a soft gray rock that is easy to carve. A wick was fashioned using moss, grass, or heather. The wick was placed in a pool of melted seal's fat or blubber, which gave off a smokeless flame. This lamp provided enough warmth that the family was able to take off their parkas. As temperatures rose inside the house, the ceiling often started to drip. To avoid a constant stream of water, the family had to constantly scrape away melting snow.

Transportation over Arctic Waters

In their land of ice and snow, it was vital for the Inuit to find ways of moving from place to place. Nearly all Inuit groups traveled great distances each year in search of better hunting grounds. Walking was an exhausting and often dangerous task because of ice and frigid temperatures. So the Inuit created two very unique methods of transportation—the kayak and the sledge.

Like the snow house, the kayak has long been considered one of the distinguishing features of Inuit society. Sleek and speedy, this lightweight boat allowed the Inuit to silently skim over the water in search of prey. To make a kayak, sealskins with the fur removed were soaked and then stretched over a whalebone frame. Seal oil was rubbed all over the boat to make it waterproof.

Each kayak was made to fit exactly one owner. About twenty feet long and three feet wide, the kayak was used for hunting seal and small whales in the waters around the Arctic Circle. The kayaker sat in a small cockpit, protected with more sealskin to keep him dry, similar to the waterproof skirts used in kayaking today. A paddle made of ivory, bone, or wood was used to propel the boat through the water.

The Inuit also used a much larger boat called an *umiak*. Nearly thirty feet long, it had a frame of whalebone with sealskin stretched over it to create a waterproof hull. The umiak could hold eight to ten people and was used primarily for whale hunting and for carrying people and their belongings from place to place.

These boats enabled the Inuit to travel quickly over the water without getting wet. To move over the snow and ice, however, the Inuit turned to another device—the sledge, or *komatik*.

Transportation over Arctic Snows

The sledge, or dogsled, was as important to the Inuit as the car is to people today. A sledge consisted of a platform resting on two runners. A typical sledge was usually around twenty to thirty feet long and maybe a foot

The dogsled made winter travel to hunting grounds possible.

Huskies

The Inuit have trained dogs to pull their sleds for more than four thousand years. The dogs they use are Siberian huskies and Alaskan malamutes, both of which are descended from wolves. These dogs have a thick double coat of fur that enables them to live outdoors in even the most frigid temperatures and conditions. During blizzards and howling winds, the dogs can curl up into tight balls and wrap their huge fluffy tails over their feet and noses and still remain warm.

Dogs have always been one of the most prized of all Inuit possessions. In fact, it would have been virtually impossible for the Inuit to survive in the Arctic without them. Without the dogs, the Inuit could not have traveled the long distances they did looking for food.

A typical Inuit family usually had around six dogs. These animals were not pets. They were treated like working family members. Before the Inuit ate their own meals, they would see to it that the dogs ate first.

Dogs were even given Arctic clothing. When the sea started to thaw, it formed sharp needles of ice on the surface. These needles could seriously cut the dogs' paws. To prevent injury, the Inuit made boots for their dogs from bits of caribou skin. Holes were cut for the dogs' claws so they could walk safely on the ice.

A properly trained dog team was necessary to keep the sledge running smoothly. The lead dog won his position by being the fiercest and strongest among his companions. The Inuit driver always walked or ran beside the sledge, keeping a constant watch on his dogs and praising them frequently. Drivers controlled their dogs with whistles or other signals.

---

high. The platform was made of animal hide, usually caribou, while the runners were built from whalebone or whatever other material the hunter could find.

The Inuit often made their runners out of frozen fish. They would simply gather together dozens of fish and form them into a long blade shape, which was then covered with sealskin. A thick paste of earth and decayed vegetation was smeared on the fish runners and allowed to freeze. This process created a hard, thin layer of ice that provided for a smooth and fast-running sled. This freezing process also solidly connected the runners to the remainder of the sledge.

The Inuit sledge made it possible for families to get to their winter hunting grounds. The sledge was heavily loaded with all the family possessions while the family walked beside or behind it. Only the smallest and youngest children got to ride on top. Nearly all Inuit, regardless of where they lived, used sledges during the winter months.

The Inuit were one of the few native peoples of North America who had to develop such extreme measures just to stay alive. According to writer George Stuart, "Equipped with everything from kayaks to the larger umiaks, and with . . . dogsleds . . . (Inuit) culture stands as the culmination of Arctic technology."[7] These devices enabled the Inuit to utilize virtually every resource the Arctic had to offer on both land and sea. Against overwhelming odds, the Inuit survived. Their successful struggle enabled them to form a way of life and a culture that sustains them even today.

Chapter 2

Hunters of the Far North

Inuit culture was based on a subsistence way of life—meaning that they lived entirely off the land. Since they lived in a snow-covered environment, it was impossible to farm or grow any kind of crops. Because of this, their way of life was based totally on hunting and fishing. Inuit hunters often traveled thousands of miles each year just to feed their families and communities.

Because their very lives depended on hunting, the Inuit had to learn to hunt in the most effective manner. According to author Jason Gardner, "The natural world was their first and foremost teacher."[8] The Inuit, for instance, learned much from the wolf, who led the same kind of nomadic life they led and ate the same kinds of food. Watching the wolf stalk its prey, the Inuit learned how to anticipate the movement of certain animals. This enabled them to ambush their prey at the most favorable places.

The Inuit also learned a great deal from the polar bear. It was the bear who showed the native hunters how to find and kill the seal. Inuit hunters learned to find the seal's breathing holes in the ice and to wait there patiently and quietly until the animals emerged.

Hunting as an Art Form

In addition, by watching the polar bear, the Inuit hunter learned how to maneuver across the ice. Walking on the frozen surface was always a dangerous task. A fall on or through the ice could easily lead to serious injury or death. For this reason, the Inuit watched the bear closely. The best way to walk, they discovered, was with their legs spread wide apart. This seemed to produce less weight on any single section of ice. They also learned to slide their feet along quickly without stopping.

Every kind of animal in the Arctic played a role in the lives of the Inuit. Because all animals were considered sacred, the Inuit always treated them with great respect. Hunting became more than just a way to put food on the table. According to writer Barry Lopez, "Hunting [was] holy. . . . And the life of [this] hunting people [was] regarded as a sacred way of living, because it [grew] out of a powerful, fundamental covenant."[9] This covenant—or agreement—between the hunter and the hunted involved tremendous responsibilities. For this reason, ceremonies and rituals were performed before, during, and after a hunt to ensure success.

With their inventory of kayaks, umiaks, and specialized tools, the Inuit, according to historian George Stuart, "utilized virtually every resource the Arctic had to offer on both land and sea."[10] In the process, the Inuit developed specialized ways of hunting and fishing and "virtually transformed those activities into an art form."[11]

Hunting the Bowhead Whale

Many of the Inuit lived near the sea, where the waters of the Arctic Ocean provided most of their food. The search for the bowhead whale was their most important activity of the year.

The bowhead whale is a large whale that lives only in the Arctic Ocean. It can grow up to sixty feet in length, is black in color, and has a flat, wide, finless back. Each spring these

The Narwhal

From the pack ice comes a loud *poooff*—an explosive noise that sounds like a steam locomotive. The Inuit are very familiar with this sound. It comes from a narwhal—a most unusual whale found only in the Arctic. Measuring up to eighteen feet long, the narwhal weighs nearly two tons and is grayish white in color with dark gray or black spots all along its body. Its most unusual feature is a spiral ivory tusk about eight feet long that juts out from the male's upper jaw. This tusk is the narwhal's only tooth. Its exact function is a mystery but scientists believe that it might be used as a weapon.

During the Middle Ages, many Europeans believed that this creature was related to the mythical unicorn—that delightful creature with one horn. A narwhal tusk, like one from a unicorn, was believed to possess magical powers. It was worth its weight in gold, and the tusks still fetch a high price in markets around the world today.

Each summer the narwhals return to the fjords and inlets on Greenland's northwest coast to feed and give birth. Only the most skillful hunters are able to successfully hunt and kill one of the magnificent animals. Currently only the Inuit are permitted to hunt the narwhal, and local regulations limit the number of animals killed each year. Out of respect for Inuit tradition, today's hunters must first strike the whale with an old-fashioned harpoon before killing it with a high-powered rifle. Meat from the narwhal is considered a real delicacy among the Inuit of Greenland.

Two Inuit whalers approach a bowhead whale, an important food source that lives only in the Arctic Ocean.

whales return from their winter homes in the south to once again swim in the Arctic waters.

The arrival of migratory birds in early April was usually the first sign that the whales were returning to the Inuit homeland. Then a few weeks later, the solid sheets of ice covering the sea began to melt and break apart. Soon the masses of ice would float away from the shoreline, opening up the seas to hunting. The breakup, or *sikuliqiruq,* occurred in early

June, as the ice on shore began to melt with a cracking sound, like gunfire.

From this time of year onward, lookouts kept constant watch for the whales while the entire village began special preparations for the hunt. Women sewed new sealskins to cover the whaling boats, or umiaks. Whale-boat captains, or *umeliks,* were given new boots to wear made of white fur and hide. These captains were usually the leaders of the various villages and held a place of honor among all the residents.

Finally, the day came when it was time to launch the boats. Crewmen would dip their harpoons in the water, a custom thought to bring success to the hunter, and proceed out to sea. As the hunters neared the whales they began to sing traditional whaling songs. Often these songs took the form of poems, remarkable for their use of symbols and images.

As the whale broke the surface the harpooner would use his skill to plunge a harpoon into the animal. The whale would typically thrash around and then dive in an attempt to elude the hunters. The wounded whale, however, would eventually have to resurface in order to breathe, because like all mammals they needed air to survive. The whale was harpooned again as soon as the hunters could see it. Once dead, the whale would be towed to shore with the help of all the boats.

The success of the Inuit at whale hunting is even more amazing when one considers the immense size of the prey. The bowhead whale is at least twice the length of an Inuit umiak and weighs well over a ton. Yet, using only handmade harpoons, the Inuit were incredibly successful in hunting this whale.

The End of a Whale Hunt

When the bowhead whale was finally dead, the crew that struck the first blow led the procession back to shore. As they neared the village, all the crewmen joined together in a great shout of joy. The women on shore sang songs while the entire village gathered to help pull the whale onto the beach.

Once the whale was on land, everyone helped with the butchering. The hunter's wife was then responsible for sharing the meat with the entire village. This sharing was based on the Inuit belief that wild animals

Harpoons

The harpoon was one of the many primitive yet extremely effective inventions that enabled the Inuit to be such great hunters at sea. The secret to the harpoon's success was a bone spear point that could be detached from the weapon. This spear point was connected to the long shaft of the weapon with strong sinew or muscle tendons made into rope. The harpoon also had floats attached to one end.

When the harpoon struck the whale or other animal, the spear point came free. This left the animal still attached to the line and floats. The floats acted as a drag and also prevented the whale from diving too deeply and escaping from the hunters. Eventually the animal would weaken and have to resurface. At this point the hunter would close in for the kill.

were no one's exclusive property and should be shared with everyone.

No part of the whale was wasted. Whalebone was used for building houses, tents, weapons, boats, and sledges, while whale oil was used for heating and cooking. Sewing needles and other small tools were often made from baleen, the hard, shiny, flexible material attached to the whale's upper jaw.

The rest of the whale was used for food, including the eyes, organs, and blood. A particular favorite among the Inuit was whale skin, which was eaten raw. It was later discovered by scientists that whale skin is extremely rich in vitamins and minerals. The meat from one whale could feed an entire village for many months.

A successful hunt usually led to a great celebration. "We have been living on the ice for thousands of years. We have developed a kindred relationship with this great animal,"[12] said one Inuk, referring to the whale. The killing of the whale is still treated with great reverence by the modern Inuit. Celebrations are held today, said another Inuk, "to let the whale know we are happy."[13]

Hunting for Seals

Fur seals are probably the hardiest of all Arctic mammals. Belonging to the family

Inuit men butcher a whale for a feast, combining sport and festival.

The seal was the second-most important food source for the Inuit.

Pinniped, which means "fin-footed," seals were the second most important source of food for the coastal-dwelling Inuit. The fur seal is a sea mammal with a sleek, torpedo-shaped body that lives along the coasts of the Arctic. It is able to survive the cold climate because its body is specially designed to handle the cold. Beneath an outer layer of fur is a thick layer of blubber that helps keep heat inside the seal's body. Like whales, seals are mammals, which must surface periodically at holes in the ice in order to breathe.

Before leaving his winter snow house, the Inuit hunter often hung a special stone or object called an amulet around his neck. This special good luck charm was believed to ensure a successful hunt. As the hunter made his way across the ice, he would often chant a special "seal song" such as this one used by the Inuit of Canada: "Beast of the sea! Come and place yourself before me in the dear early morning!"[14]

While some seals were hunted from kayaks, most were killed at their breathing holes. Finding the seal's holes, or *aglus,* was one of the most difficult tasks facing the hunter. In the cold Arctic, most of the tiny holes quickly froze over, making them almost impossible to see from a distance. The Inuit, therefore, relied on their dogs to sniff out the holes in the ice.

A slightly different technique was to insert a thin ivory rod through the ice. When a seal approached, the rod would start to jiggle. Without actually seeing the seal, the hunter could thrust his spear or harpoon into the hole and kill the seal.

Using the Seal for Nourishment and Clothing

Once the seal had been killed, the hunter and his friends would pull the seal out of the water and onto the ice. The hunter then made a small cut in the animal's abdomen and removed the liver. This was a special treat that the hunter shared with his companions while the meat was still warm. A special plug made out of animal bone was used to close the spear wounds on the seal's body. These plugs held in the seal's blood, which was an important part of the Inuit diet.

A hunter waits for a seal to surface at a breathing hole.

Skinning and butchering the seal was a woman's task. She often used her special knife, the *ulu,* to accomplish this job. In order not to offend the soul of the dead seal, special rituals were performed. Holding the seal's mouth open, the woman offered it a drink of water by sprinkling a few drops inside. This ritual was always performed and was based on a belief that the seal's soul might be thirsty.

Once the hunter arrived at a breathing hole, he would place nets below the ice. Some hunters carved themselves a snow seat in the ice, where they covered their feet with fur, sat down, and waited. As the seal approached his breathing hole, it would become trapped in the net, making it easier for the hunter to spear or club the animal to death.

As with the whale, the Inuit used every part of the seal in one way or another. Sealskin, because it is waterproof, was commonly used in making the coverings for umiaks and kayaks. Seal oil, made from blubber, was an important source of cooking and heating fuel. The blubber was simply cut into small pieces and placed in some kind of container. Within a few days it turned into oil. In addition, seal meat was a vital part of the Inuit diet. A real favorite was blood soup, which was served warm and relished throughout Inuit society. Seal's blood could also be made into a kind of chewing gum for Inuit children.

Hunting the Walrus

Another animal that came from the sea and played a crucial role in Inuit life was the walrus—a huge seal-like animal with tusks. During the winter and spring, these animals drift along on large floating fields of ice in the Arctic Ocean. Even in dense fog, hunters could easily locate them by following the sound of their bellowing.

Most walruses were killed on the ice as it was too dangerous to hunt them on open water because of their massive size. A walrus's most prominent feature is its tusks, which can grow to over three feet long. The animal uses its tusks to defend itself when attacked or threatened. An angry or wounded animal could easily injure a hunter or damage a boat.

Harpoons were used to kill a walrus and it often took several men to bring one down. Walrus hide was often used in making the skins of Inuit boats while ivory from the

Hunting Birds

The Inuit hunted many different kinds of birds along the Arctic coasts, but the two most common were ducks and geese. These two birds, along with many others, summered in the Arctic where insects and nesting sites were plentiful. Hunting and killing birds was usually the first step in a young hunter's education. In addition to eating the meat from the larger birds, the Inuit made great use of the eggs.

Inuit hunters used a wide variety of methods to kill the birds. Traps and nets were fashioned by some individuals, while other hunters made use of bows and arrows.

One of the most effective and unique tools, however, was the bola. This was a device made of animal sinew that was then braided into lengths of about thirty inches. Ivory or bone weights were attached to the braids and then fastened to a bone handle. Grasping the handle, the hunter whirled the bola around his head and flung it into a group of birds. As it flew through the air, the weights wrapped around a bird and brought it down.

A walrus is butchered for winter meat. All parts of the animal will be used.

tusks was used to make tools. The meat, while sometimes eaten by the Inuit, was most often used to feed their dogs. Walrus bones were widely used to make harpoons.

Hunting and Using the Caribou

One of the most magnificent sights on the Arctic tundra is the annual migration of the caribou. Every spring these large North American deer move out of the forests and onto the open tundra to raise their young. In the autumn they head south again—a round-trip journey of thousands of miles.

Thickly furred, the caribou are ideally suited to the Arctic. Their hooves spread out to act like snowshoes, making it easier for them to move across the snow-covered tundra. Caribou also have hollow hair follicles that allow warm air to be trapped within them, thus providing extra warmth for the animal. Found from western Alaska to western Greenland, caribou were called *tuktu* by the Inuit. This word means "the animal that paws through snow for food."

Of all the animals in the Arctic, it was the caribou that played the most important role in the hunting life of the inland Inuit. Indeed, for the Inuit, the caribou was a department store. Nearly everything they needed could be obtained from the caribou.

Caribou meat was an important part of the Inuit diet. Caribou heads were boiled to make a kind of stew or soup, and the leg bones were cracked to get at the marrow inside, which was then roasted, boiled, or eaten raw. In addition, caribou skin was used to make everything from tents to clothing. Sewing thread was made from caribou sinew while sewing needles and other small objects were made from the bone. Caribou antlers were used to make harpoons, arrows, and snow goggles.

The Inuit used a number of different methods for hunting the caribou. Most frequently, the animals were simply speared from kayaks as they swam in the small lakes and streams that dotted the Arctic tundra. To accomplish this, the Inuit built a large V-shaped corral out of rocks near the water's edge. The Inuit knew that the caribou preferred to cross streams at narrow or shallow points. As the caribou moved down the stream towards shore, the Inuit simply encircled the trapped animals and killed them. The hunters' weapon of choice was a spear, made of a long bone with a sharp point at the end.

Caribou were hunted because they could provide food and materials for clothing, thread, and arrows.

Fishing

The Inuit, in addition to being great hunters, were also excellent fishermen. Salmon was the fish most often caught, but whitefish and trout were also available. An adult salmon spends most of its life in the sea or ocean, but lives in freshwater streams when young. In the spring and summer the adult salmon swim great distances of up to one thousand miles in an effort to return to the same river where they were born.

Like many other peoples before the age of technology, the Inuit used devices called weirs to improve their success at fishing. An Arctic weir consisted of two dams built across a shallow and rocky part of the river. The first dam had a good-sized opening, allowing the fish to swim inside. The fish then entered a V-shaped funnel that led into an area that was blocked by a second dam. Once

trapped, Inuit women, who played the primary role in fishing, could easily spear the fish.

The Inuit also developed a remarkable spear called a leister for catching fish. A long handle made of bone ended in a central bone point, which was flanked on either side by barbs. The point speared the fish while the barbs prevented it from escaping.

The Inuit had great respect for the fish as they did for all animals and living things. When the first fish returned in the spring, the Inuit often held special ceremonies to welcome the fish home. Inuit beliefs also prevented them from cleaning the fish near the water. This was because rivers and streams were considered holy places. Inuit who broke this rule would find themselves having bad luck in future fishing expeditions.

Inuit fishermen spear salmon with pointed, barbed leisters.

Another very effective hunting technique was the stampede and ambush. Using bows and arrows made out of bone, this method of hunting was highly developed and required the participation of the entire village. Inuit hunters would set up a line of cairns—or piles of rocks—along the trails that the caribou traveled. Women and children from the village hid behind the rocks and made loud noises or howled like wolves in order to scare the caribou into stampeding. Waiting with their weapons, the men then killed the animals as they rushed by.

Unlike other animals the Inuit hunted, the caribou was butchered on the spot instead of being taken back to camp. The caribou heads were always cut off first and placed in a separate pile. The Inuit performed this ritual to prevent further suffering of the caribou's soul. The hunters were then given the choicest pieces of meat, usually the nose or tongue. Once again, the women were given the task of butchering and skinning the animals.

Hunting and Using the Polar Bear

Polar bears are the largest and most powerful animals in the Arctic. They are very solitary, preferring to hunt and live alone, except when mating and breeding. Polar bears are noted for their thick undercoat of heavy fur, which is protected by another layer of fur called an outercoat. This outercoat is made up of long "guard" hairs that stick together when wet. This enables the bears to stay warm and keep their skin dry in the ice and snow of the Arctic.

In many Inuit groups, the killing of the polar bear, or *nanook,* was considered the greatest of all hunting challenges. This was due, in part, to the bear's great size. Many weighed over one thousand pounds and when standing were anywhere from eight to ten feet tall. The polar bear was also an animal that the Inuit respected above all others. Many Inuit believed that the bear was their cousin because, among other things, it walked upright. The Inuit of Alaska, in fact, tell the following story about the first bears.

Long ago on the shores of the Arctic Ocean, an Inuit woman lived. . . . She already had several children but then one day she gave birth to two more. These children, who were twins, were very odd indeed. One was covered with long white fur while the other had a skin of brown fur. The mother did not want these two children as they looked very different from her other kids. She took them far away from her igloo and left them alone. As soon as she was gone, the white furred child got up and ran down to the beach and on out across the frozen sea. The brown child did not follow his twin but rather headed in the opposite direction towards the mountains and forests. And there they have lived ever since. But people do not call them men. They are known as Nanook or polar bear and grizzly bear.[15]

Hunters traveled by dog sledge while tracking polar bears. Once a bear was within sight, the dogs were released. They rushed at

Three Inuit women stretch and dry a polar bear hide in the bright Arctic sun.

the bear from all sides, barking furiously. While the dogs were keeping the bear busy, the hunter moved in with his spear or harpoon. Aiming at the bear's exposed chest and rib cage, the hunter threw his weapon and hoped for the best.

Every part of the bear was put to good use. Polar bear fur was occasionally used in clothing but it was usually considered too heavy to wear except on the coldest days. Polar bear meat was considered a great treat. One part of the bear that the Inuit never ate, however, was the liver, which was considered poisonous. It is now known that this organ contains toxic (deadly) amounts of vitamin A.

Even with modern firearms, the Inuit today consider hunting the polar bear a huge challenge. Only the very best hunters are chosen for the hunt, which is still considered the supreme test of a young man's courage. In some parts of Greenland, young men are not considered worthy of marriage until they have taken their first bear.

The Mighty Grizzly

In other parts of the Arctic, the Inuit also attached great significance to another mighty bear—the grizzly, which they called *aklaq*. If a hunter was successful in killing one, he often hung the bearskin on his door. Whoever

Food Preservation

When animals were killed, it was the responsibility of Inuit women to butcher them. They were also responsible for preserving the meat for year-round eating.

After the animal was skinned, the best cuts of meat were often eaten on the spot. For instance, after a whale hunt the members of the community often stuffed their cheeks full of whale blubber while they worked on the animals. Afterward a special feast was held to celebrate the successful hunt. The Inuit literally ate until they could eat no more. It wasn't at all unusual for some men to eat as much as eight pounds of raw meat at one sitting.

The remainder of the meat was sliced into thin strips by the women and then hung or laid out in the sun to dry. After drying out for several days, the meat was then preserved in one of two ways. Sometimes it was packed away in the bladders of dead animals while seal or whale oil was added to keep it from spoiling.

More often, another method of storing food was used. Arctic iceboxes—or *sigluaq*—were built by digging down in the ice to a depth of one foot. This hole was usually located near an Inuit village and was covered with moss, sod, or animal skin to provide insulation. There in the frozen ground, the food stayed fresh and ready for use all year round. Storing food in this way was essential during the winter when food and game were scarce.

Meat was preserved by cutting it into thin strips and hung in the sun to dry.

entered the home was immediately aware of the homeowner's bravery and skill.

Killing a grizzly prior to the time when hunters had firearms was quite an accomplishment. A hunter's only weapon was a strong bone-tipped spear. After waiting in ambush, the hunter leaped out at the bear, startling it and causing it to rear up. The hunter would quickly dart under the bear's front paws and plant his spear in the ground. As the bear came down to crush the hunter, the bear landed on the sharp point of the spear. The man would then dive out from under the bear and finish killing the animal.

Neither bear—polar or grizzly—was usually the primary target of Inuit hunters. They were simply too dangerous for anyone other than the greatest of hunters.

Where Are the Animals Now?

The bowhead whale, seal, walrus, caribou, polar bear, and grizzly bear were once numerous in the Arctic. The Inuit treated them with respect and killed only those animals they needed in order to feed and clothe themselves. With the coming of the white man, things began to change for the Inuit and the animals on which they depended.

The bowhead whale, for instance, was heavily hunted from the 1700s to the early 1900s by European and American whalers and nearly became extinct. It is now an endangered species and is protected by international restrictions. The Inuit, however, have been given permission by the International Whaling Commission to legally hunt a small number of bowhead whales each year for food.

Beginning in the sixteenth century, fur seals were hunted by professional sealers almost to the point of extinction. Using clubs and harpoons, white hunters killed thousands of them every year. In 1911, Canada, Russia, Japan, and the United States signed an agreement to protect the fur seal from further hunting. This policy had a devastating effect on the Inuit, whose way of life depended on the seal.

In 1909 the United States banned the killing of the walrus, but the law was seldom enforced. Today's law allows only Alaskan natives to hunt the walrus and then only in limited numbers.

At one time as many as two million caribou roamed North America. By the end of the 1800s many of the big herds were gone, wiped out by white hunters with rifles. Many of these herds have since been restored, but they face danger today from the effects that oil drilling in the Arctic are having on their migration routes.

Polar bears have vastly decreased in numbers during the twentieth century. Global warming has caused significant changes to the ice on which the bears thrive, while pollution is threatening their very existence.

The grizzly bear has fared only a little better. These animals are still hunted in both Alaska and Canada, although the number of grizzlies remaining seems stable at this time.

Chapter 3

Family and Community

The Inuit have always centered their way of life around family and community. The harsh living conditions in the Arctic made this a necessity. As an unidentified Inuit woman told explorer Knud Rasmussen in 1923, "Up here where we live, our life is one continuous fight for food . . . and a struggle against . . . snowstorms and sickness."[16] Individuals simply could not survive on their own in such an unforgiving environment. Cooperation was needed in nearly every aspect of Inuit life. The Inuit, therefore, tended to travel and live in small groups made up of several families.

The term *band* is more accurate than *tribe* to describe these early Inuit groups. According to writer Paula Younkin, "Bands are more typical of hunting societies like the Inuit because their leadership did not rest with chiefs or other hereditary leaders."[17] Instead, those individuals with exceptional skills often served as informal leaders. In many cases, these were the best hunters of the group and would serve as leaders during one particular hunting season.

A man, his wife, and his children formed the basic unit of Inuit society. Grandparents, brothers, sisters, nieces, nephews, aunts, and uncles often lived with the family or in nearby homes. All members of the Inuit family were important and were considered valuable participants in family and community life.

The Inuit community was organized around these family groups, and each community member carried out specific tasks according to age, sex, and status. Men, for example, were responsible for building houses, making boats and tools, and hunting. Women took care of skinning and butchering, gathering vegetation, fishing, preparing food, and making clothes. With little cooking and housecleaning to do, Inuit women spent most of their time sewing new clothes and repairing old ones. Being a hunter's wife was hard work. Because of this, an Inuit man regarded his wife as his most prized "possession."

Most activities required cooperation and sharing among the different households. This

An Inuit woman demonstrates the slow process of dressing an animal skin.

was and still is the primary characteristic of Inuit social life. With no written law, the Inuit followed traditional rules of conduct and lived in an amazingly close-knit and law-abiding society.

Marriage

Marriage held a place of special significance among the Inuit. Parents usually arranged marriages while their children were still quite young. In some Inuit groups, it was the girl's parents who made the marriage proposal by giving the chosen youth a parka or knife. In other societies it was the prospective groom who proposed by giving the young woman new garments made by his mother.

People in Inuit society married early. Girls were usually around the age of thirteen or fourteen, while boys might be a couple of years older. Sometimes there was a trial period during which the young man actually lived with the family of his intended wife. If he was a good hunter and got along well with everyone, the family generally approved the marriage. The couple then announced to the community that they were husband and wife. Without any kind of specific ceremony, the newlyweds simply returned to the young man's family home and lived there.

Some husbands had more than one wife, but this was quite unusual among the Inuit. A far more frequent occurrence was a practice called wife sharing. Occasionally, a man's own wife would be unable to go with him on a hunting trip because of pregnancy or illness. Without a woman to cook, dry his clothes, and process animal hides, a hunter could be in a very difficult situation. The man often asked a close friend or neighbor if he could borrow that man's wife for the hunting season. His own wife would be left with the friend or neighbor. These exchanges were not permanent and happened only during the hunting season.

Coming of Age in Inuit Society

The Inuit, unlike so many other Native American groups, did not have any kind of public ceremony to welcome a child into adulthood. For the Inuit teenager, adolescence was handled in less formal ways. Boys might put on different clothing once their voices changed or have their lower lips pierced.

Teenage girls, on the other hand, might be tattooed. Tattoos were a sign that a girl was ready to marry. Typically the tattoos were three blue lines placed below the lip and reaching to the chin. These were very painful to get. Tattoos were made by pulling a sooty string or a hair dipped in plant juice just under the surface of the skin. Pricking holes into the skin using a sharp bone could also make the marks. These marks were thought to greatly enhance a female's beauty.

There was some ceremony attached to a girl's first menstrual period. In many communities the girls were confined to a special hut during this time. They were required to wear a special hood of caribou skin that was used to protect their eyes from the glaring sun. The sun was believed by many Inuit to be particularly harmful during the time of the menses. In addition, the girls had to obey certain restrictions such as not eating or touching any red meat.

Every Inuit was expected to marry at a young age. A girl's first menstrual period marked her readiness for marriage, while boys had to be old enough to build a house and hunt.

Because there were more men than women in Inuit society, there was often fierce competition and occasionally violence between male rivals for a particular woman. In fact, it was not unusual for young men to actually kidnap other men's wives. A husband then faced several options.

He could, of course, take his wife back by force. This usually led to long feuds and bloodshed between rival families. Inuit society frowned on this kind of behavior. The husband could also offer to let the man keep his wife in exchange for goods. The final option—and the one most preferred by the Inuit—was to ignore the situation and hope that at some point the wife would return.

Divorce, though not common, was allowed among the Inuit. A woman could divorce her husband at any time by simply leaving home and returning to her parents. Men could essentially do the same thing, although the husband might end up having to provide for his former wife by giving her meat that he had hunted.

Children

Most Inuit marriages were not considered official until the couple produced a child. Until that point, the two individuals could "split up" without offending the community. Children were extremely valued in Inuit society, especially boys, who were warmly welcomed for their future potential as hunters.

Inuit women usually gave birth, not in a bed, but while kneeling on a bed of dried grass or moss. Some delivered their own children, but the majority had the help of older female relatives. Following the birth of a child, the placenta, or afterbirth, was buried for religious reasons and a diaper of caribou hide or moss was placed on the infant. The mother then remained in a special "birth hut" with the baby for four or five days.

An Inuit couple poses for a photograph. Inuit couples were traditionally married without a ceremony.

A baby sleeps peacefully in the amaut, *or hood, of the mother's parka.*

A child spent the first few years of life being carried around on the mother's back. This was accomplished with the use of an *amaut*—a hood in the mother's parka. Mothers nursed their babies and carried them on their backs until the children were three years old. When the child grew too old to nurse, a portion of a seal's intestine was prepared for use as a baby bottle.

New parents would carefully examine their children for birthmarks, mannerisms, or spe-cial physical traits that might provide a clue as to what the child's name should be. For example, a child who resembled a dead relative might be given that person's name. A child's birth name was often so sacred that it was never said out loud.

As children grew older they were often given nicknames. The Inuit believed that all names carried great power and also acted as guardian spirits. Most Inuit wanted to acquire as many names as possible during their lifetime

A sense of closeness shows on the faces of an Inuit family. Families are central to Inuit culture.

because this meant that many spirits would protect them. When a newborn baby cried repeatedly, the Inuit took that as a sign that the infant wanted a different name.

The mother usually had the primary responsibility for raising children. She was there with them on an everyday basis while the father was away for long periods of time hunting. When home, Inuit fathers did play with their children, hugging and rubbing noses with them. At the age of four or five, many Inuit boys began to follow their fathers around camp, watching and studying everything their fathers did. By the age of seven, girls were expected to start helping their mother by learning how to sew, cook, and keep the household running.

Adoption was very common among the Inuit. A childless couple might adopt their nephew or an older woman might take in a grandchild. Neighboring families often took care of each other's children. And occasionally those families with lots of children might give one to a family that had none. All these adoptions were permanent. The Inuit frowned upon and even scorned those parents who changed their minds.

Community Life

The Inuit always lived within some kind of community. This could be as small as just a few families or as large as three hundred people. In a typical village all the houses were grouped around a large community center, called a *kashim* in Alaska and a *karigis* elsewhere. There the Inuit would gather to sing, dance, tell stories, feast, or hold religious ceremonies.

Sharing tasks and responsibilities was the basis of community life for the Inuit. Each person had a role to play in the community and freely shared whatever talents they might possess. This spirit of sharing was nowhere more evident than in the Inuit practice of providing food for everyone. When food was scarce, for example, an Inuit would be more than willing to give away his last bite of nourishment to someone who needed it more.

The Inuit valued hospitality highly, and thus it is not surprising that visiting and feasting were the focus of community life. Guests usually announced their arrival by shouting into the tunnel entrance or merely entering the home. Some Inuit groups allowed both sexes to eat together, while others separated them. It was often a point of pride to serve the guests the best pieces of meat in the house, and guests could simply doze off if they became sleepy.

Cat's Cradle

The Inuit loved to play games of every kind. Cat's cradle was one of their favorites. In this game, individual players would use their fingers to shape figures out of a circle of sinew thread. The natives were expert at this process and could make elaborate and complicated figures of animals and other objects. Inuit adults and children could amuse themselves with this game for hours at a time.

Cat's cradle can be played very easily today by young and old alike. The ends of a long piece of string are tied together and the loop is placed around the fingers of both hands, leaving out the thumbs. Reaching across the middle finger of the right hand, a person would catch hold of the string that runs across the opposite palm. The hands are then pulled apart. The process is repeated with the middle finger on the left hand. The string is hooked and pulled across the right palm and the hands are once again pulled apart. The string has formed a simple basketlike enclosure, which is called a cat's cradle. From this point on, a person merely continues to cross the strings and form other shapes.

Mealtimes for the Inuit were not scheduled but occurred whenever people got hungry. Most food was simply served raw, but meat could also be boiled or smoked over the soapstone lamp. Fresh water was obtained from melted snow or ice. And in the summer, berries and edible roots were added to the diet, where available.

Despite the fact that the Inuit were a happy and community-minded people, there was seldom any public touching or hugging. Nose rubbing and nose kissing were much more common. According to historian Ron Fisher, "An Inuit hunter kissed his wife only on the nose. The Inuit believed that kissing on the mouth was a disgusting and dirty habit."[18]

Of all Inuit relationships, the male song partner was perhaps the most interesting and unusual. Song partners were often close friends who traveled and hunted together. The two would come together frequently in ceremonial houses where they would sing and rub noses to show how much they valued each other's friendship.

Nearly every man and woman in the Arctic was some kind of an artist. The Inuit saw little difference between making things that were useful versus making things that were beautiful or religious. Instead, all of these qualities were combined when making even the most ordinary objects. Carved figures were made for both decorative and religious purposes. Many small carvings of different figures have been found at archaeological sites throughout Canada, Alaska, and Greenland. No one today is really sure what some of these represent.

A craftsman carves an intricate design in ivory using a bow-drill.

Nonviolence

Although the Inuit have dozens of words for snow, they have no word for war. Since surviving in the Arctic was a battle in itself, the Inuit could not afford to waste time and effort in large-scale, organized conflicts with one another. The Inuit, unlike the prairie or desert tribes to the south, were not at all warlike. They were simple hunters and fishermen who did not even make weapons for war. Usually cooperation, not conflict, was the rule.

Rather than a fixed group of formal laws, each Inuit community developed its own customs and informal rules of conduct. These "rules" were passed down through the generations by word of mouth and all community members were expected to follow them.

Violence among the Inuit themselves was often prompted by ancient feuds. Anyone who felt they had been badly treated by someone else was expected to take revenge against the wrongdoer and his family. A male relative of a murder victim, for instance, was entitled by Inuit custom to kill either the murderer or one of the murderer's close relatives.

Quarrels or conflicts between two individuals were often settled in singing contests called "public song duels." Each man made up songs that insulted the other and would sing them at community gatherings. Using suggestive dance movements, the men would sing and shout at each other until both were exhausted. The man whose song was the funniest or the most insulting was declared the winner.

Punishment, Inuit Style

Perhaps the most frequently used punishment against "criminals" was public sham-ing. A thief, for example, might be made fun of or even ignored by the community. Because the Inuit valued membership in the community so much, this shaming often resulted in a positive turnaround in the behavior of the lawbreaker. For those whose acts were of a more serious nature, such as murder or repeated crimes, banishment from the community was the punishment imposed. This usually resulted in death because an individual could not survive in the Arctic alone.

From time to time a person might display a more bizarre kind of violent behavior. Temporary bouts of craziness—or Arctic hysteria—were not uncommon. Most people suffering from this problem would tear off all their clothes while running around shouting and yelling obscene words. After getting tired out, the person would usually collapse on the ground and begin crying. Most of the Inuit blamed supernatural forces for these strange episodes. Scientists today believe that the stress of living in the Arctic darkness may have caused the problem.

Perhaps because life was so hard, Inuit children were allowed to play freely and were seldom scolded. Indeed, many Europeans believed that the Inuit spoiled their children by not punishing them. Inuit parents, however, felt that wisdom and good sense would come naturally as the children grew into adulthood. They believed that many of their childhood games would prepare them for adult responsibilities.

Mockery in one form or another was generally considered sufficient punishment for

A craggy cliff provides an adventurous play area for a group of children.

most children. Quiet or unspoken forms of correction were preferred to loud shouting or verbal abuse. Yelling at a child too much, the Inuit believed, could make a child "deaf" to reasoning later on in life. Even spanking was better than loud reprimands. According to an unidentified Inuk, "Spanking hurt the skin but the constant yelling hurt the spirit."[19]

Storytelling

The Inuit, like native peoples everywhere, used stories to teach values and to explain the mysteries of the world around them. Today when children ask "why?", parents are able to explain things from a scientific or a traditional viewpoint.

Thousands of years ago the Inuit explained things based on stories that had been passed down orally from one generation to the next.

Here is a creation story from the Inuit of Alaska that has been retold by author Paula Younkin: "The Great Raven created the world. One day, Raven dropped beach peas on the bare earth and from each pea sprang a full-grown man. Raven then shaped the clay into pairs of animals and finally a woman for the first man. The peopling of the world soon followed."[20]

The World Eskimo-Indian Olympics

Today, every July, thousands of natives from all over Alaska gather in Fairbanks to participate in the World Eskimo-Indian Olympics. Begun in 1961, the event is four days long and features traditional games that test strength and endurance. It also provides an opportunity for many different native communities, including the Inuit, to come together and celebrate their unique cultural heritages.

The games include such diverse events as the greased pole walk where participants try to maneuver safely across a slick pole to reach the finish line. Men and women's blanket toss, one of the Inuit's favorite games, is also featured. Another interesting contest involves a tug of war. Instead of pulling on a big rope across a pit filled with mud, this game involves looping a piece of sinew around the participants' ears. Contestants also bounce across the floor on their knuckles in an event called the knuckle hop. Additionally, there is competition in Indian and Eskimo dancing, drumming, and singing.

Each year a panel of judges chooses a native queen to reign over the games. In recent years, attendance at these Olympics has been increasing as more and more native Alaskans participate. The games are one more way that the original inhabitants of the Arctic are striving to preserve their cultures.

A participant at the World Eskimo-Indian Olympics stretches for the ball in the one-foot high kick event.

Games

The Inuit, young and old alike, loved to play games. During the long winter months many families and communities spent hours together engaged in various forms of competition. Indoor games included fingerpull, a game similar to arm wrestling. Two opponents faced each other with their right toes touching. They hooked the middle fingers of their right hands and attempted to pull each other off balance. The one who lost his balance was, of course, the loser.

Nuglugaqtuq was another favorite winter game. A large piece of bone with a good-sized hole cut in the middle of it was used for this game. This bone was hung from the ceiling of the snow house or community house. Players tried to poke a stick through the hole while the bone was swinging back and forth. As players became more experienced at this game, additional holes were cut, each one with its own point value. Inuit families could play this game for hours while forgetting all about the blizzard that might be raging outside.

A favorite winter game for Inuit girls in western Alaska was storyknives. Inuit girls gathered around the quilliq and told each other stories just as children do today while gathered around a campfire. As they were telling the tales, the girls would draw pictures into their knives with a sharp bone. The knives then became storyknives and could be used at later gatherings to repeat these stories.

During the summer the Inuit young engaged in outdoor sports like children everywhere. Kickball and touchball were both popular on the tundra. Both games were played with a ball of sealskin that had been stretched and then stuffed with hair or grasses. To play touchball, the Inuit hung the ball from the ceiling or from a tall bone or ivory pole. Lying on their backs, children

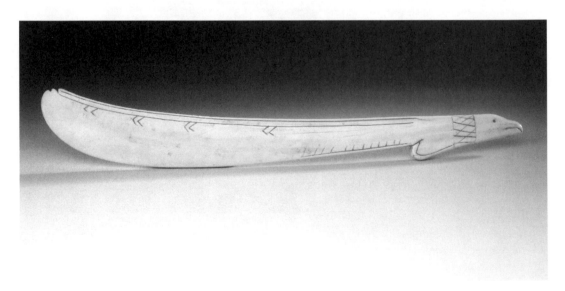

Pictures carved on storyknives like this one kept tales alive for another day.

tried to reach the ball with one or both feet. The game could also be played standing up, with children jumping as high as they could to touch the ball. Whoever could reach or kick the highest won the game.

One of the Inuit's favorite games was the blanket toss. A blanket made of walrus skin was held at the edges by several people and pulled tight. One person got on the blanket and was thrown high up in the air. Many Inuit could do fancy twists, somersaults, and tricky turns. Hunters who used a blanket toss to spot game in the distance handed this game down to their children. The Inuit call this game *nalukataq* and it is still played in many parts of the Arctic. No doubt, the trampolines that children play on today are based on the Inuit blanket toss.

Whether they were hunting, playing games, or feasting, the Inuit lived a peaceful and happy life. They respected their environment and learned to live within it. They depended upon one another and shared freely in a spirit of togetherness. Their possessions were few—usually only a few items of clothing, a few tools and weapons, an occasional carved toy, and their precious dogs. Despite these few items, the Inuit believed their lives were rich and bountiful. The land had provided all they needed or desired.

Chapter 4

Religion and Ritual

The Inuit lived a rich spiritual and religious life that was characterized by numerous rituals, celebrations, and religious rules, called taboos. Their world was a complicated one made up of spirits, all of whom were respected and feared. They believed that every living being and object had a spirit and soul. In addition, the Inuit believed that the land on which they lived was sacred. For that reason, the land and the animals had to be respected and preserved for future generations to enjoy. These beliefs form a kind of spirituality called animism.

The Supernatural

The Inuit believed in a wide variety of spirits and supernatural beings. These beings took the form of gods and goddesses, ghosts, monsters, and mythic figures. Each group of Inuit had its own specific figures of worship, but they usually all centered on a supreme being or god.

For many Inuit, this supreme being was known as Sila. An unidentified Inuit elder once defined Sila as a spirit who supported "the world and the weather and all life on earth." He went on to state,

> Sila is a spirit so mighty that what it says to humankind is not through common words but by storm and snow and rain and the fury of the sea; all of the forces of nature that people fear. But Sila has also another way of communicating—by sunlight and the calm of the sea, and little children innocently at play. . . . No one has seen Sila; this spirit is at once among us and unspeakably far away.[21]

In other parts of the Inuit world, different spirits controlled the world. One was the Spirit of the Air who was responsible for wind and weather and also gave all living things breath. Another was the Spirit of the Sea who was in charge of all sea creatures and their souls. Finally there was the Spirit of the Moon who influenced the souls of all land animals.

Another spiritual being was Narssuk, a gigantic baby who controlled the wind and snow. The Inuit believed that Narssuk hated humankind because it was always snowing and very cold in the Arctic. Another being was Tatqeq, the moon spirit. She could bring good fortune to a hunter and could also help women get pregnant. Thunder and lightning, according to historian Paula Younkin, were caused by "two girls shaking [animal] skins and striking a flint in fury at their ill-tempered father."[22]

The Inuit also lived in fearful respect of wandering animal ghosts and numerous other supernatural forces. These supernatural beings took many shapes and forms, from tiny mischievous dwarfs to huge ogres and terrifying monsters. A large number of myths and legends surround these creatures. One group of Inuit living along the coastal areas of the Arctic, for instance, believed in little beings about one foot high who dressed in tiny parkas and lived in underground houses along the seashores.

In Greenland, the most frightening of all creatures were horrible and dangerous

The Story of Sedna

For many Inuit, Sedna was one of the most important goddesses of all. The editors of the Reader's Digest book *America's Fascinating Indian Heritage* report this story of Sedna and how the sea animals came into being.

Once there was a beautiful girl named Sedna who married a seagull and went to live in a country of gulls. Once there, Sedna became very unhappy and called out to her father to come rescue her. The father arrived, killed Sedna's husband, and fled with his daughter in a boat. The gulls were quite angry and flew after them, causing a great storm to occur.

Hoping to calm the gulls, the father threw his daughter overboard, but Sedna clung to the edge of the boat. He cut off her first finger joints and tossed them into the sea, where they became whales. Then he cut

off the second joints, which soon turned into walruses. Her third joints became seals.

The storm soon subsided, for the gulls believed that Sedna had drowned. But instead she had taken up a home on the bottom of the sea where she became a sea spirit and the mother of all sea animals. She sent out the animals to feed mankind, but also at times withheld them, causing the people to starve if they broke certain taboos.

To make peace with Sedna, an Inuit shaman would go into a trance and then send his soul flying across the sea. He would arrive at a great whirlpool that marked the entrance to Sedna's home. There, the shaman would try to calm the goddess by combing her hair. This was important and pleasing to Sedna because she was unable to perform this task, due to the loss of all her fingers.

The strange-looking tupilak, *half raven and half child, was thought to possess demonic powers.*

demons called the *tupilak.* The Inuit believed that evil sorcerers who wanted to do away with their enemies created these beings. After combining parts of dead humans and dead animals, the sorcerer sang special songs to bring them to life. It was believed that once the monster came to life it would wait underneath the ice and then sneak up on unsuspecting victims. Images of the tupilak were often carved in ivory and kept in secret places to ward off evil spirits. Today these carvings are sold as souvenirs.

The Inuit tried to live a life of harmony with all the forces around them. Inuit life centered around keeping these forces happy in ways prescribed in great detail in their ancient traditions.

The Shaman

The shaman, or healer, was one of the most important members of Inuit society. This person served as the religious or spiritual leader of the community and acted as a vital link between the human world and the realm of spirits. All members of the community had great respect for the shaman and for shamanic abilities.

Inuit shamans, men and women who were believed to have contact with special spirits who appeared to them in dreams or visions, were credited with possessing extraordinary powers. They could, according to traditional Inuit accounts, "shake the earth, walk on clouds, make themselves invisible, raise the dead, [cure the sick], and give off sparks from their own bodies."[23]

By far their most important power was the ability to "fly." Shamans reportedly could fly off to visit the gods and goddesses, where they were said to retrieve lost souls and obtain special information. Inuit frequently reported seeing shamans in flight. Their faith in shamanic tales of far-off places was nearly unshakable.

The Inuit shaman could, for instance, "fly to the moon" to get a baby for a childless couple. Since the moon was associated with fertility, this trip was usually successful. If hunting was bad, the shaman could fly to meet with a sea deity to find out what the people needed to do to improve their success.

Because the Inuit believed that all illness was caused by spiritual problems, one of the shaman's most important jobs was curing the

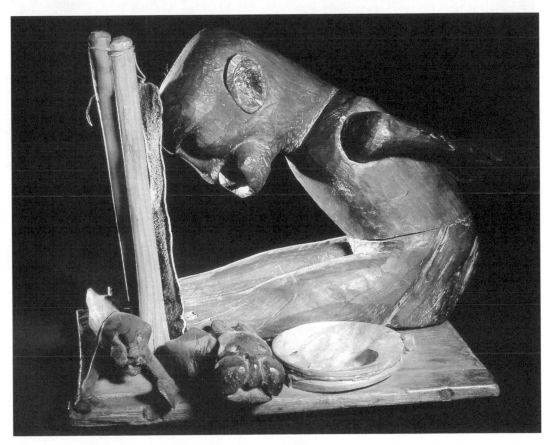

Shamans, like the one depicted in this carving, served as religious and spiritual leaders of the Inuit community.

sick. Healing usually took place in a public ceremony. As the sick person was brought before the shaman, the individual was expected to confess to any breaking of Inuit taboos. In cases where an "evil spirit" had entered the person's body, the shaman would suck or blow on the diseased part, hoping to remove the offending "object" and throw it into the fire.

Many illnesses, the Inuit believed, were caused by the person's soul wandering away or having been stolen by an evil sorcerer. It was up to the shaman to retrieve it by making an "out-of-body" journey to another level of reality while in a deep trance. Essentially, the shaman's spirit left his body and "traveled" until the lost soul was found. Once the soul had been recovered, the shaman blew it back into the sick person's head or heart.

Shamans also acted as village doctors. Traditional shamans, for instance, applied fat to burns, lanced infections, and even set broken bones. They used urine to clean open wounds. All households kept a special pot to hold urine for this very purpose. Urine has been used by many cultures over the ages to treat wounds in this fashion. No one is quite sure why urine is so effective, but many scientists suspect that some of the acids in urine kill harmful bacteria.

Becoming a Shaman

It was indeed a great honor to receive a "call" to become a shaman. This call usually came through a dream or special vision. According to historian and mythologist Joseph Campbell, "strange and unknown beings came and

An Inuit shaman takes evil spirits out of a sick boy's body.

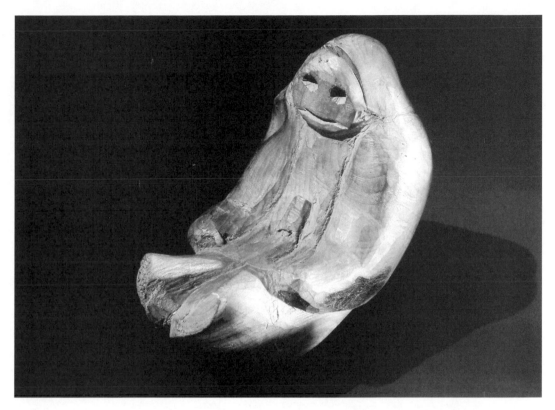

Figures like this one represented shamans and their ability to communicate with spirits.

spoke to [a young man] and when he awoke he saw all the visions of his dreams. . . . Soon it became evident to all that [the young man] was destined to become a shaman or *angakoq*."[24]

In the depth of winter when the cold was the most severe, a young man or woman was placed on a small sledge just large enough for the "apprentice" shaman to sit on. A specially appointed instructor, usually an older shaman in the village, then carried the shaman-in-training far from home. On reaching the appointed spot, the instructor built a tiny snow hut just big enough for one person to sit cross-legged inside. The instructor then picked the shaman trainee up and carried him or her to the hut.

According to Joseph Campbell, "No food or drink was given him. He was told to think only of the Great Spirit [or God] and of the helping spirit that should presently appear."[25] Five days later the instructor brought the young person a small drink of lukewarm water. Another fifteen days would pass before the elder would return. Again, the young person received a drink of water and, this time, a very small piece of meat. At the end of another ten days, the instructor returned and brought the shaman home.

Campbell writes, "During the thirty days the young man thought only of the Great Spirit and tried to keep his mind free of all memory of humans and everyday things. Toward the end of his time, a helping spirit or *toornaq* came to him . . . [and] became his special spirit."[26]

For the next five months the young shaman was kept on a strict diet and could not have sex. The fasting was repeated periodically as long as the shaman lived. The Inuit believed that such fasts were the best means of attaining knowledge of spirits and hidden things.

Joseph Campbell writes also of a young woman named Kinalik who became a shaman. "She was hung up to some tent poles in the snow and left outside for five days. It was midwinter with intense cold and frequent blizzards but she could not feel the cold because the spirits protected her."[27]

These kinds of initiations were practiced by the Inuit all over the Arctic. In fact, similar methods were used by different cultures all across the globe. If the shamans could survive these severe tests of faith, then their powers of healing were assured.

Taboos of Birth and Death

The Inuit believed that the spirit world was populated by beings who could either behave or stir up trouble. To keep the spirits from becoming angry, the Inuit lived by a strict set of religious "rules" called taboos. These taboos governed all aspects of their life.

A Shaman Speaks

Each Inuit shaman had his or her own helping spirit to assist with healing and the retrieval of souls and other shamanic work. Joan Halifax in her book *Shamanic Voices* presents a description given by an Inuit shaman, Aua, to explorer Knud Rasmussen.

"My first helping spirit was my namesake, a little aua. When it came to me, it was as if the passage and roof of the house were lifted up, and I felt such a power of vision, that I could see right through the house. I could see in through the earth and up into the sky. It was the little aua that brought me all this inward light, hovering over me as long as I was singing. Then it placed itself in a corner of the passage, invisible to others, but always ready if I should call it."

The shaman went on, "An aua is a little spirit, a woman, that lives down by the sea shore. There are many of these shore spirits [whose] pants are queerly short and made of bearskin. Their feet are twisted upward and they seem to walk only on their heels. They are bright and cheerful when one calls them and they resemble sweet little live dolls. They are no taller than the length of a man's arm."

People gather for a traditional funeral, one of many customs followed after a death.

Childbirth, for instance, was surrounded by taboos. A pregnant woman was not allowed to stay in the family snow house because she was believed to be unclean. Instead, she was isolated in another small house nearby where she stayed until several days after the baby was born.

Many taboos also had to be followed when a person died. For the first four to five days after death, the family of the deceased could do no work. Others in the camp could not comb their hair, cut their nails, feed their dogs, or clean their cooking lamps. To do otherwise could cause the dead person's soul to suffer and linger too long on earth.

The body also had to be removed from the person's house in a special way. This taboo involved cutting a hole in the wall of the house and taking the body out of this new opening. It was considered unlucky for the body to be taken out the front door. A large number of native groups, including the Inuit, believed that the soul might linger in the house and cause problems for the surviving family members.

Taboos for Hunters

Taboos were also very important for hunters. Women were not allowed to scrape a caribou skin while a caribou hunt was in progress for fear this would offend the animals' spirits. Nor did the Inuit boast or brag about their hunting conquests, as this might anger the spirits of the animals they hunted. At the moment of a kill, the hunter actually apologized to the animal and asked forgiveness.

Prior to a whale hunt, the Inuit observed many rites of purification. All the equipment was cleaned, new clothes were made, and the hunter always slept apart from his wife. Eye contact with a woman was forbidden before a hunt. Doing otherwise was considered a waste of a hunter's good eyesight and might cause the hunter to miss when he threw his harpoon.

When a polar bear was killed, its skin had to be hung inside the snow house for five days. This was the length of time that the Inuit believed the bear's soul remained on the tip of the spear that killed it. The Inuit would also hang presents on the bear's skin to satisfy the dead animal's soul.

The Inuit believed that it would be foolish not to respect the spirits of the animals they hunted. If they didn't follow certain acts of courtesy to the dead animal, these same creatures would not allow themselves to be hunted in the future. In addition, bad luck would come to the hunter and his family. All animals were offered food and water after death as a courtesy and a sign of respect. The more important the animal was for food, the more rituals and taboos were associated with the hunt.

An unidentified Inuit hunter once explained the failure of polar bears to appear for hunting season in this manner. "No bears have come because there is no ice. There is no ice because there is too much wind. There is too much wind because we mortals have offended the powers and spirits."[28]

And in the words of another Inuit hunter,

The greatest peril of life lies in the fact that human food consists entirely of souls. All the creatures that we have to kill and eat, all those that we have to strike down and destroy to make clothes for ourselves, have souls, souls that do not perish with the body. The spiritual duty of the hunter then is to appease those souls so that they don't revenge themselves on us.[29]

Death

The Inuit believed that the human soul lived on after death. If the proper death taboos were not observed, these souls could conceivably turn into evil spirits, who might hang around camp and cause dangerous problems. These dark, angry spirits were known as *tarraks*. If, on the other hand, the taboos were correctly observed, the departed soul would go to live peacefully in one of several afterworlds.

Two of these worlds—one high in the sky and one deep within the earth—were places of great beauty and pleasure. The souls of brave hunters and women of great beauty were admitted to these special places. For the lazy and for those who repeatedly broke the taboos, there was a different world awaiting them. This place was just below the surface of the earth and was a very sad place where souls often went hungry.

Skulls are revealed in an Inuit grave. The Inuit believed that the soul remained in the body several days after death.

The Inuit also believed that when a person died, the soul split into two parts. The personal soul of an individual was the part that went to these various afterworlds. The other part of a person's soul was called the "name soul." This soul remained on earth until a new baby was born that could be given its name along with all that person's skills.

When a person died, the Inuit believed that the soul usually remained in the body for four or five days. At the end of the five-day mourning or grieving period, the body was placed on a sledge and driven far away. Because the ground was frozen so much of the year, the body was often left right on the ice.

In other areas of the Arctic the body was sewn into a large skin, taken far from the community, and placed on the ground facing east. The body, along with that person's belongings, was then covered with rocks.

Special Ceremonies

The Inuit held many sacred and special gatherings. These festivals and other ceremonies were used to celebrate upcoming or successful hunts and as opportunities for the Inuit to come together to sing and dance. Such events were a combination of spiritual renewal and just plain fun. Singing and dancing were a special part of Inuit life, for each song and dance had significance and meaning.

In the western part of Alaska the Inuit held a celebration called the Bladder Festival each year. In this area of the world, young men entered adulthood by killing their first seal. After returning from a successful hunt, the young man went directly to the ceremonial hut, or *kashim*. Singing one of his family's secret hunting songs, he entered the hut with his prize. The seal's meat was divided among the village elders while its skin and bladder were hung from the ceiling of the hut.

Masks and Charms

Masks made to look like humans, animals, or spirits played an important role in Inuit celebrations. In many cases the designs on the masks were based on specific visions that an individual Inuk had. When the mask was worn, the wearer temporarily took on the spirit of the character on the mask. For instance, if the mask depicted a wolf, the Inuk wearing it would "become wolflike" and howl. Women also wore masks, but theirs were called "finger masks" and were worn on the fingers. These were tiny replicas of what the men wore, and the women who used them made flowing hand movements.

When Inuit women wore finger masks (pictured) they took on the spirit of the character of the mask.

Amulets or special charms were worn or carried by nearly everyone. These charms could be anything from a feather to a tooth. The Inuit believed that these charms protected the wearer from evil spirits. They could be hung around the neck, attached to clothing, or used to decorate tools and hunting equipment.

The Inuit believed that the seal's soul resided in its bladder. All hunters carefully collected and stored in the ceremonial hut the bladders of the seals they had killed. The bladders remained there in the kashim until the Bladder Festival was held, usually around the winter solstice in December.

The young man who had killed his first seal had to follow very strict taboos until this festival was held. He could not eat any kind of seal meat and was forbidden to remove his clothes at night. Both he and his mother could not eat anything at all during the five days of the festival itself.

As the Bladder Festival began, all of the animals' bladders were inflated with air and painted in bright colors, using dyes taken from berries. Members of the community told stories and there was usually singing and dancing. The singing and drumming were done softly because the Inuit believed that loud and unpleasant noises were offensive to the animals' souls.

On the last night of the festival the village shaman gave a speech to celebrate the seals that had been killed. Everyone then gathered up the bladders and followed the shaman down to the sea to release the seal spirits. The bladders were ripped open and thrown into the sea. Occasionally the shaman was lowered into the icy water in order to talk directly to the souls as they departed.

The young hunters who had killed their first seals joined in the celebration. After each one had released his own animal's soul, he stripped naked and ran along the beach, regardless of weather. With this celebration, the young man's childhood was considered officially over and he was free to marry.

Chapter 5

The Coming of the White Man

For thousands of years the Inuit believed they were the only people in the world. They had endured some of harshest conditions on earth and survived, while in the process developing a unique and remarkable way of life. Starting around the end of the sixteenth century their society began to be threatened by forces they could not control. A succession of explorers, fur traders, whalers, missionaries, white government officials, and eventually oil companies moved into the Arctic. These groups would have a profound and devastating impact on the Inuit and their way of life.

The Explorers

European explorers were drawn to the Arctic in the hopes of finding an all-water route from Europe to Asia so they could take advantage of the riches of the Orient. Prior to the sixteenth century, merchant ships had to sail from Europe, south down the west coast of Africa, around the tip of that continent, and then north and east to Asia. This route took many months to successfully complete.

In the late 1500s explorers began to sail west toward the Arctic in an effort to find a shorter way. The discovery of such a route, called the Northwest Passage, could dramatically shorten the time it took ships to make the voyage to Asia.

The first explorer, other than the Vikings, to make contact with the Inuit was Martin Frobisher, an Englishman. In 1576, Frobisher passed the southern tip of Greenland and headed northwest until he entered a broad inlet that he hoped was a passage to the Far East. His ship, the *Gabriel,* was almost immediately approached by a group of Inuit in a boat. The rowers seemed friendly and were invited on board.

When the explorers began making threatening gestures, the Inuit fled, taking five captives with them. These prisoners were treated well and eventually released unharmed, but not before Frobisher had taken his revenge. The explorer and his men responded by capturing several natives. Rather than releasing them, Frobisher returned to England with them. There, they were presented to Queen

The Vikings

For over four hundred years, from the eighth well into the twelfth century, the Vikings took the world by storm. In search of land, gold, silver, and slaves, these explorers and warriors from Norway, Sweden, and Denmark ruled the seas. They raided all across Europe and were the first explorers to reach parts of North America.

The Vikings were also the first Europeans to settle in the Arctic and to actually have contact with the Inuit. Erik the Red, a Viking from Norway, encountered the Inuit when he founded a colony in Greenland in A.D. 983. The Viking explorers generally discounted the natives, calling them *skraelings,* or barbarians.

A successful trade in skins, furs, and ivory between Greenland and Northern Europe grew from these early contacts. But the Vikings never learned to live off the land as the Inuit did. And, as the Inuit ventured closer and closer to the Viking settlements in search of sea mammals, confrontations and violent outbreaks began to occur. This hostility with the natives was one of the many factors that ultimately led to the Norse abandoning their settlements in Greenland in the fourteenth and fifteenth centuries. Trade problems, scarcity of food, and the bitter cold also played prominent roles.

This apparently was one of the few times in history that a native people was victorious in a confrontation with Europeans. The Inuit survived and their culture and society persisted in Greenland.

The ruins of a Viking church in Greenland, where Europeans and Inuit first encountered one another.

Martin Furbisher, the first English explorer to make contact with the Inuit.

Elizabeth I. An unnamed British historian described them as "primitives who ate only raw meat and used neither table, stool or tablecloth."[30] Unused to the climate of England and exposed to new and deadly diseases, the Inuit all died within months of arriving.

Further European exploration in the Arctic during the sixteenth century failed to find a shorter route to China and, after 1616, the voyages ceased for nearly two hundred years. They resumed again in 1819 when Englishman John Franklin led the first of several overland expeditions to explore the Arctic coast of North America. He traveled more than five thousand miles by canoe and brought back a wealth of information about the area.

During Franklin's stay in the Arctic he used an Inuit guide named Tatanoyuk. Tatanoyuk, one of the most respected of all guides, also served for many years as an interpreter. One of his actions saved Franklin and his men from an attack by hostile Indians. Tatanoyuk was able to explain that Franklin meant no harm, and the British group was allowed to safely continue its journey.

In 1821, two other Englishmen, William Parry and George Lyon, tried again to find the Northwest Passage. When their ships became trapped in the ice, they were befriended and helped by the Inuit. Lyon later wrote, "I verily believe that there does not exist a more honest set of people than the tribe with whom we had so long an acquaintance."[31]

Despite these and many other efforts to find a shortcut to Asia, the explorers were unable to find the Northwest Passage. It would not be until the early twentieth century that polar explorer Roald Amundsen, a Norwegian, finally discovered a way through the Arctic to the Pacific Ocean.

The written records from these European explorations all describe the voyagers' amazement at the ability of the Inuit to survive in the Arctic. Most of the explorers quickly realized that to stay alive, they would have to rely on the natives of the Arctic. For that reason, most of the nineteenth- and early twentieth-century expeditions treated the Inuit in a respectful and peaceful manner.

After these explorers mapped different routes through the Arctic, other white men followed in their footsteps. These men came not for adventure, but for reasons of greed.

Exploring the North Pole

It must have been hard for the Inuit to understand why polar explorers like Robert Peary wanted to go to the North Pole. After all, the pole was just some invisible geographic point where the ice was too thick to even think of hunting seal. This lack of understanding, however, didn't stop the Inuit from escorting the explorers to the pole. The Inuit respected these men for their bravery, their leadership skills, their respect for the land, and their willingness to learn.

The polar explorers also respected the Inuit and learned much from them. Robert Peary, one of the greatest Arctic travelers of all time, quickly won the Inuit's confidence and friendship. Staying with them for an entire year before venturing farther north, Peary learned how to build a snow house, how to drive a dogsled, and how to dress for warmth and survival.

While there remains some controversy over who was the first to reach the North Pole, most historians believe that it was Peary. Trained as a surveyor and engineer, Peary made eight polar expeditions. Working closely with the Inuit, he was brought closer and closer to his goal with each trip. On February 22, 1909, Peary set off again. When he finally reached the pole on April 6, 1909, he was accompanied by his manservant (Matthew Henson, a black man who made seven polar trips with Peary), four Inuit, and a couple dozen huskies.

Arctic explorer Robert Peary gained the respect of the Inuit while living among them.

The Fur Traders

During the seventeenth through the early twentieth century there was a great demand for fur clothing throughout Europe. Mink, beaver, fox, wolf, bear, seal, and other furs were very popular, but these animals had been hunted and trapped on the European continent until they were near extinction there. Reports of large numbers of furbearing animals in the Arctic brought a number of hunting expeditions to the New World.

White trappers and merchants quickly realized that the Inuit were experts when it came to hunting these animals. Europeans and Russians soon began a brisk trade with the natives. Furs were exchanged for coffee, tea, sugar, tools, and rifles. With these new weapons, the Inuit could kill more animals.

Trading posts were set up all across the Arctic. These posts became the center of a vast fur-trapping industry that soon spread throughout the region. Most traders were fair, but many others were not. In Alaska, for instance, the Russians treated the Inuit like slaves, forcing them to leave their homes and work long hours without pay. Thousands of natives died on the Alaskan islands as a result of starvation, disease, and mistreatment.

Dependence on the trading post began to change the Inuit way of life. For the first time

European fur trappers and merchants set up trading posts all over the Arctic, which resulted in the Inuit's dependence on them.

in their history they were no longer relying on the land to provide all their needs. Now many of the Inuit were trapping strictly for trading purposes and not for food. They began to rely more and more on the goods they could obtain from trading. This led many Inuit to move into areas where the trapping was good. Unfortunately, some of these places could not support their traditional hunting practices. The result was starvation and hard times for the Inuit.

A Canadian report documented this situation: "One native wanted to give a written statement saying the place was no good for hunting, and [that] they wanted to go north . . . where there [was] good hunting but [they] were afraid the white men would not like it. All the natives of this camp complained of hard times."[32]

A far more serious problem caused by contact with white fur traders was the Inuit's exposure to strange and deadly diseases. Before contact with Europeans, the Inuit's overall health had been excellent. They were far more likely to die from exposure to the elements or from animal attacks than from disease. After contact with the white man, this began to change.

Unlike the Europeans, the Inuit had no natural resistance or immunity to certain diseases because they had never been exposed to them before. Tuberculosis, smallpox, measles, influenza, and whooping cough spread throughout the native villages like wildfire. Historians estimate that as a result, in the artic, nearly half of all the Inuit perished. In one area of the Arctic that had been home to two thousand Inuit, new diseases caused the population to

Whaling ships rushed to the Arctic to meet the demand for goods that whales provided.

drop to around thirty in about forty years. Many of these diseases continued to destroy large numbers of the Inuit population well into the twentieth century.

The Whalers

Big whaling ships came to the Arctic from thousands of miles away in the 1800s. Hunting whales was big business for a variety of reasons. In the early nineteenth century there was no electricity. Oil was needed for light and heat, and the majority of this oil came from the whale. Whales also provided baleen, a flexible material used in making a wide variety of products from women's corsets to fishing rods. Even the fluid found in the whale's intestines, called ambergris, was an essential ingredient in perfume. When the whalers discovered that during the summer months the Arctic waters were filled with whales, ships headed there by the hundreds.

The Inuit found the whalers to be a strange people. They praised the whalers' ability to produce valuable articles and implements, but they usually laughed at the Europeans' inability to clothe, feed, and protect themselves. The whalers, on the other hand, according to writer Barry Lopez, "found little to value or respect in the Inuit. They believed that the Inuit were a people to be taken advantage of, to be treated like children, but definitely not to take seriously."[33] The Europeans, in fact, called them "yaks."

Because they believed that the sea belonged to everyone, the Inuit initially welcomed the whalers. Soon their attitude changed as they realized that these men were slaughtering whales by the thousands, not for food but for money. This concept was hard for the Inuit to understand, for they were a people who respected the environment and the animals within it. They had lived for centuries in balance with the whale and now they were facing starvation because of hunting done by others.

During the last half of the 1800s, overhunting of whales by Europeans led to a dramatic shortage of the animals. By the early 1900s these whalers with their modern equipment had killed more whales than the Inuit had killed in the centuries before the whalers arrived.

This decline in whale numbers meant that one of the Inuit's most important sources of food was endangered. The problem was made worse by the fact that towards the end of the whaling period, the whalers turned to hunting other, smaller marine animals such as beluga whales, walruses, and seals. Before the whalers were done, they had killed almost all the wildlife that the Inuit traditionally depended on. By the time the whalers finally left the Arctic, many of the Inuit were starving.

Missionaries

While the explorers, fur trappers, and whalers brought some changes, it would be the missionaries who would have perhaps the greatest impact on Inuit culture during the late nineteenth and early twentieth centuries. According to historian Paula Younkin, the missionaries' efforts to "civilize the heathens did more to extinguish Inuit culture than the hundreds of years of exploitation by others had. The missionaries came not to claim riches but to change the people."[34]

The missionaries saw the Inuit as a backward and primitive people. They believed that the natives needed to give up their traditional ways of life and adopt a white way of living. The missionaries, acting in good faith, held the common belief that native peoples everywhere needed to be assimilated or absorbed into the more civilized white culture. This policy meant the Inuit would be encouraged—and forced if necessary—to give up the very things that had made them unique and enabled them to survive for thousands of years.

The first missionaries to arrive were the Lutherans in 1721. They settled in Greenland, determined to civilize and Christianize the natives. It was not long before other missionaries followed. These early church people went from village to village setting up temporary churches in snow houses and tents. They invited the Inuit in for tea and began to talk to them about Jesus. The fact that the Inuit had never tasted tea and couldn't understand a word that was being said only reinforced the missionaries' belief that the Inuit were a very backward people.

The missionaries lumped the complex taboos and supernatural beliefs of the Inuit as pagan—or non-Christian—practices and ideas. From the beginning, the missionaries worked to change the beliefs of the Inuit. They did this by imposing their own belief system on the Inuit and by forbidding the natives to follow many of their spiritual practices. Gradually the leadership of the shamans was destroyed. Inuit taboos were ridiculed,

while native songs, dances, and ceremonies were discouraged—and eventually forbidden.

The missionaries also set up schools for Inuit children. The white teachers did not allow the youngsters to speak in their native tongues, and those who did so were punished. This practice further weakened traditional Inuit ways of life.

Government Intervention

Until the early part of the twentieth century, the white governments of the United States, Canada, and Greenland had, for the most part, ignored the Inuit. Suddenly more and more outsiders were becoming interested in the Arctic because of the gold and other mineral

A well-attended Easter Sunday service, one of the many changes in Inuit culture resulting from contact with Christian missionaries.

discoveries made there. These new outsiders demanded government protection. As the century opened, the Canadian government sent Royal Canadian Mounted Police—Mounties—into the Arctic and, for the first time ever, the Canadian Inuit had to live by a system of white people's law.

Schools run by the government soon replaced the missionary ones. The children were taught "white history." In the words of an unidentified Inuk, "We were taught that the Arctic lands remained undiscovered until the Europeans arrived."[35] Thousands of years of Inuit history were simply erased. It has only been in the last twenty or thirty years that Inuit schools have provided students with a more accurate curriculum.

In 1945 the Canadian government officially took over the schooling of native groups. Children were sent to faraway boarding schools where they were told they needed to learn how to act and behave in a "civilized" society. Inuit children, who had been raised on seal, caribou, and whale meat, were introduced to a diet of packaged, processed, and cooked food. They had to eat with forks and knives and were forced to sleep between sheets on thin mattresses and beds. For the Inuit, accustomed to the ancient ways, it was a drastic change.

When these young people returned home they were often unable to communicate with their parents. In addition, they were incapable of living off the land, because they had forgotten or been "untaught" the traditional ways. Even when they had skills for modern employment, prejudice and lack of jobs kept them from being hired.

The Alaskan Inuit were also required, until 1976, to send their high school students to distant boarding schools. In that year a court ruling ordered that any village that wanted a high school could have one. Earlier, the Bilingual Education Act of 1967 in the United States required schools to offer classes in native tongues for the first time. Unfortunately, several of the Inuit languages had already disappeared. Dr. Michael Krauss, the leading Alaska expert on language, has predicted "that by 2055 most of Alaska's native languages will be extinct."[36]

Moving the Inuit

For thousands of years the Inuit had lived in their traditional hunting villages, moving with the herds of animals they hunted. Beginning in the 1950s, white governments began a program of forced relocation. The reasons for this move are still debated among historians, although the reasons given at the time included native starvation and poor medical care. The Inuit were not consulted, and their "ownership" of the land was virtually ignored.

This decision to move the Inuit from their traditional villages and hunting camps to modern towns and small communities left behind a legacy of crime, unemployment, alcoholism, and suicide that the natives still struggle with today. While different from the reservation system used in the United States, these new locations were, as Inuk John Amagoalik recalls, "like landing on the moon."[37]

Nowhere was the struggle more intense than in Canada. In 1953 the Canadian government ordered the transfer of all families in northern Quebec to two new settlements only

Government-run schools taught children "white history" with curriculum that omitted history of the Inuit.

nine hundred miles from the North Pole. The government explained the move of more than a thousand miles as an attempt to increase the Inuit's hunting opportunities. The Inuit had only tents for shelter and little equipment to deal with life in a new and much harsher climate.

Thousands of other Inuit were moved into permanent communities elsewhere. Natsiq Kango, a young Inuit woman, described what happened to her family. As author John Geddes relates,

> Her family along with other Inuit hunting clans scattered around the southeastern tip of Baffin Island (a Canadian

island in the Arctic Ocean) had recently been persuaded by federal authorities to settle elsewhere. One day a Royal Canadian Mounted Police truck arrived at the beach not far from their new home. A Mountie stepped out and shot her father's dogs. The slaughter denied her father the option of taking his family by dogsled back to their traditional winter hunting ground.[38]

While tragic, this was not an isolated experience for the Inuit.

According to the editors of *Encyclopedia Britannica,* "This transplanting of their traditions and lifestyle caused great social

Birthing Practices in Canada

For generations Inuit babies were born at home with the help of older women. In the 1950s the Canadian government outlawed the practice of home birth. Remote nursing stations were established and white nurses were given the responsibility for delivering babies. The Inuit weren't happy with this because of the language problem and the prejudice displayed toward their local traditions. But at least the deliveries were done within the community.

Then in 1982 the government passed a new law that required pregnant women to fly thousands of miles to regional hospitals to give birth. There the woman would live in a boardinghouse until she was ready to have her child. Her husband and children were not allowed to accompany her. The food, climate, environment, culture, and language were all unfamiliar and most of the women were extremely frightened. A woman usually waited several weeks before delivering— alone and not understanding what anyone was saying.

In very recent years, however, things are finally beginning to change for the better. Inuit women have formed various committees with the purpose of taking back many of the responsibilities for their own health care. Now hospitals provide interpreters and at least allow a woman's family to accompany her. Slowly the Inuit are returning to a community- and home-based system of childbirth.

upheavals and made the Inuit, as a whole, lose their self-esteem and faith in their own culture."[39] The men and women essentially felt useless. For hundreds of years the men had been hunters feeding their families while the women made the clothing and raised the children. Now, the white governments were demanding that the Inuit forget their traditional practices and adopt the white man's modern way of living.

Chapter 6

Entering the Twenty-First Century

As the Inuit enter the twenty-first century, they struggle to overcome the problems caused by the effects of forced relocation. They are also faced with a need and desire to preserve their traditions and history amidst the growing problems of the modern world. They are trying to find ways to balance their former nomadic hunting lifestyle with the "ways of the white man." In addition, they are fighting to protect their land and wildlife from a growing array of modern problems.

Despite these many issues and concerns, the Inuit have made several great strides forward in recent years. With the recent creation of an Inuit homeland in Canada and the successful reclaiming of land in Alaska, the Inuit look to the future with hope and courage.

The Growth of Tribal Movements

Much of the hope and promise of today is the result of the growth of tribal movements. The term *tribal movement* refers to the actions that Native Americans everywhere are taking to keep their cultures alive. In the last

thirty to forty years the Inuit have acted with great courage and ingenuity as they have fought to reclaim what is rightfully theirs.

Inuit tribal movements started as a response to new interest in the Arctic areas by the governments of the United States and Canada. This outside interest began during World War II with a massive military buildup in the Arctic because of the threat of a Japanese invasion. Many Inuit families were forced from their land. A few found jobs with the military, building airstrips, radio stations, and barracks. Unfortunately, once the bases were built, these jobs for the Inuit disappeared. The Inuit were not consulted about the use of their land and, from this, concluded that the outsiders considered them an inferior group of people whose opinions did not matter.

Outside intervention continued during the Cold War of the fifties and sixties. During this time the United States and Canada were greatly concerned about a possible nuclear missile attack from the Soviet Union. A large number of radar stations were built stretching from Alaska to Greenland. These stations made up the Distant Early Warning, or DEW, Line. Their purpose was to closely monitor the Communist nations of the Soviet Union and China in order to warn of potential missile attacks. Again, the Inuit were not consulted.

The Inuit were ignored once more in 1968 when oil was discovered in the Prudhoe Bay area of the Alaskan Arctic Circle. It was one of the greatest oil discoveries in history. Work on a pipeline from there to Valdez in southern Alaska began in 1974 and was completed three years later at a total cost of eight billion dollars. The Trans-Alaskan Pipeline, a system of pipes used to carry the oil, runs for a length of about eight hundred miles. The pipeline crosses some of the roughest country in the world—and the Inuit's traditional homeland.

Radar line stations like this one make up the Distant Early Warning Line and stretch from Alaska to Greenland.

The Trans-Alaskan Pipeline

When oil was discovered in the Alaskan Arctic in 1968, the United States decided that a pipeline would be needed to carry the oil south. However, two significant problems had to be overcome in building the pipeline. The first was the frozen tundra. Building anything on the tundra was difficult because it was impossible to dig very deep into the ground. For that reason, most of the pipeline was built above ground. In some areas the pipes are high enough to permit wild animals to pass underneath.

The second problem was the extreme cold. In frigid temperatures, concrete and steel can become extremely brittle. To ensure a free flow of oil, the pipeline is protected by heavy insulation.

The Trans-Alaskan Pipeline is continually checked for cracks that could lead to destructive leaks. While no leaks have yet occurred, the tundra suffered great damage during construction. Heavy machines crushed fragile soil and killed plants. Some massive areas of bare earth have no chance of recovery. Roads and railways that were built to move workers and supplies also seriously affected the habits of many native species of wildlife.

At Prudhoe Bay today the tundra is lit up for miles around as flames shoot from natural gas plants that are nearly eight stories high. Bulldozers the size of houses grind back and forth constantly on the nearby roads. The contrast between this area and the rest of the Arctic is startling. Prudhoe Bay is noisy, cluttered, and polluted while the rest of the Arctic is clean, breathtakingly beautiful, and largely untouched by human hands.

With so many outside forces moving into the Arctic, the Inuit began to come together to talk about what was happening to them. They had several purposes in mind. The first was to protect their land rights and traditional ways of life. Second, they hoped to solve many of the social problems that were adversely affecting their lives. Finally, they hoped to revive and preserve their cultural heritage for future generations.

The Inuit in Alaska quickly realized that the discovery of oil was a perfect opportunity for them to begin a push for governmental recognition of their land rights. The Inuit, together with other native groups in Alaska, organized and petitioned the U.S. government. In their presentation the natives argued that Russia's sale of Alaska to the United States in the nineteenth century was actually illegal. Thus, the land had not belonged to Russia but to the Alaskan native peoples. The Inuit knew they could not stop the efforts to develop the oil fields, but wanted instead to stake a claim to their rightful share of the profits.

The Trans-Alaskan Pipeline runs through Inuit land, spurring claims on the profits the pipeline provides.

The Inuit found surprising support from the large oil companies that had begun to put pressure on Congress to reach an agreement. The oil companies realized that they could not start drilling until the matter was settled, nor could they begin the construction of the pipeline. These powerful oil company executives added their voices until Congress was forced to take action.

In 1971 the U.S. Congress passed the Alaska Native Claims Settlement Act. Alaskan natives were awarded ownership of over 44 million acres of land and given nearly 1 billion dollars for selling their title to additional Arctic land. This money went into regional and village corporations throughout Alaska, while the land was divided among many different native groups.

Nunavut

In the early 1970s an Inuit organization called the Tapirisat of Canada was established to protect Inuit cultural and individual rights. In 1976, members of the Tapirisat went to see Canadian prime minister Pierre Trudeau and made a proposal for an Inuit land claim and the creation of an Inuit homeland to be called Nunavut. Over the next twenty-plus years, negotiations and discussions with several different prime ministers made slow but steady progress. In June 1993 the Canadian government passed the Nunavut Act. The creation of Nunavut was perhaps the most daring step that any nation had ever taken to satisfy the needs of one of its native populations.

Shortly before the official opening of Nunavut, another history-making event occurred in Canada. In a ceremony in Ottawa on January 7, 1998, Minister of Indian Affairs Jane Stewart delivered a statement of apology for the decades of government abuse and racist policy-making. She went on to express Canada's regret for the policies that had caused such tragedy and disruption to the native way of life. She spoke of how Native Americans had been deprived of their rights; of how their land had been seized; and of how the natives had been forced against their wishes to adopt European ways. For the first time in history

The Greenland Inuit Win Home Rule

Erik the Red, a Viking from Norway, was the first outsider to encounter the Inuit when he founded a colony and named it Greenland in A.D. 983. Greenland is the largest island in the world and is considered part of North America. It lies in the North Atlantic and in places is only ten miles away from Canada. Most of the country is located above the Arctic Circle and is covered with thick ice. There are a number of U.S. military bases on Greenland, and these are a major part of the North American defense system.

Nearly all the residents of Greenland are descendants of the Inuit, many of whom intermarried with Danes. The natives there speak Greenlandic, a form of the Inuit language. Many of the Inuit follow their old ways of life in settlements in the far northwest, while others live in towns on the southwest coast.

From 1380 to 1953, Greenland was a colony of Denmark. In 1953 it became a Danish province, and the Inuit there were finally given citizenship and the right to vote. In 1979 the people of Greenland won home rule from Denmark. This gave them the right to regulate their own taxes, control their own education, and enact their own hunting and fishing regulations. Denmark, however, would retain control of foreign policy and the police force.

a white government had apologized to its native people.

A year later, on April 1, 1999, the creation of Nunavut became a reality. "In a blaze of fireworks beginning just after midnight, the new territory of Nunavut was born," wrote reporter Habeeb Salloum. "The long struggle of Northern Canada to have their own homeland had come about not by revolution and violence but after fifteen (long) years of discussion between the native people of the north and the Canadian government."[40]

The ceremonies started with the lighting of the quilliq—the traditional Inuit oil lamp used to heat the snow houses of the past. Native food was served at a great feast while the new legislators wore ceremonial costumes. And, in the first session of the new Nunavut government, the members sat on a traditional Inuit sledge.

Prime Minister of Canada Jean Chretien attended the celebration, stating that, "This is indeed a great day for the people of Nunavut and for Canada. On the eve of the new mil-

Representatives of the Inuit participate in the ceremony that marked the birth of the Nunavut nation.

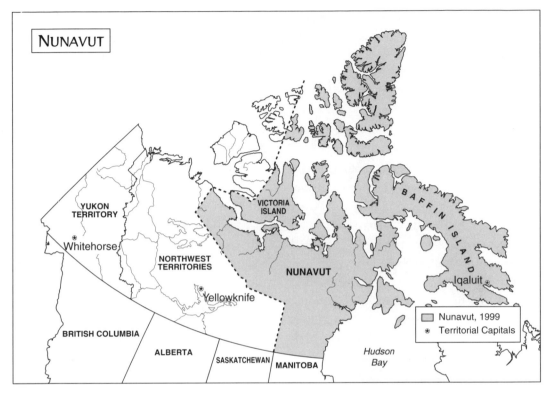

lennium we are showing the world that respect for diversity is an essential and enduring aspect of our history and our future together."[41]

Comprising 20 percent of Canada's landmass, Nunavut lies entirely within the northwest Canadian part of the Arctic. If it was a country it would be the world's thirteenth largest. The Inuit make up more than 80 percent of the population—nearly 26,000 natives who are spread out over the huge territory in fewer than thirty towns. The largest town and the capital of Nunavut is Iqaluit, which has a population of 4,200.

National Geographic writer Michael Parfit described Nunavut in the following way. "Traveling among the towns of Nunavut was like flying from planet to planet across empty space. I would leave one tiny cluster of boxy, government built houses and fly for hours across icebound bays, glaciers (and) frozen swampland before the next little village showed like a handful of pebbles on the horizon."[42]

While the Inuit now have a native government, they will still work closely with the Canadian government. They have seats in the House of Commons but also have their own legislature, much like the individual states do in the United States. There are no political parties in Nunavut. All decisions must be made by general agreement. In the words of Paul Okalik, the first premier of Nunavut—and also the first ever

Inuit attorney—"We have regained control of our destiny and will now determine our own path."[43]

Facing the Problems of a Modern World

The leaders of Nunavut also inherited many serious problems. Because of the Inuit's relocation from their homeland and other factors, their culture had been severely damaged. According to a 1996 government survey, "Over one third of the Inuit lived and depended on welfare and less than 15 percent of adults had graduated from high school."[44]

In addition, the suicide rate was found to be six times higher in Nunavut than in the rest of Canada. According to Sheila Levy, who helped organize a suicide hotline, "Suicide touches everyone here. When you talk to the kids at the school, they all have friends or relatives who have died this way."[45] In addition, infant mortality, homicide, alcoholism, and drug use are all significant problems in Nunavut.

One of the economic problems that the Inuit face today is the phenomenally high cost of living in the Arctic. This is true all over the Arctic, not just in Canada. In the past the Inuit had no need for money because of their practice of trading and sharing. When the natives were moved into communities, money suddenly became a necessity. Instead of being able to find everything they needed on the land, the Inuit discovered they needed money to buy fuel, food, tools, and other items. The Inuit essentially were forced to exchange their self-sufficient life of hunting, trapping, and fishing for one of dependency.

Money was hard to come by. Since there were far more Inuit than available jobs, poverty became commonplace among the natives, and many were forced to rely on the welfare system. There is little to no unemployment, however, for the whites who live in the Arctic. They are the administrators, managers, bosses, and supervisors and are usually paid well and live comfortable lives.

In contrast, the Inuit, if they are employed at all, usually work in dull, low-paying jobs that are seldom full-time. This makes for low self-esteem among the Inuit, especially the young. Unemployment and dependence on the welfare system do little to remove Inuit feelings of inferiority and inequality. In many communities, the rate of unemployment has reached as high as 80 percent.

Food is also extremely expensive because of the high cost of flying or shipping it to the Arctic. Food costs far more than prices that U.S. and Canadians residents pay for the same items. For instance, a five-pound bag of potatoes that sells for $1.49 in the south costs over fifteen dollars in the Arctic.

Health Care and Travel Challenges

The difficulty in obtaining medical help continues to have an impact on the Inuit. A person in Nunavut, for instance, is four times more likely to die by accidental death than the average Canadian. That same person is also eight times more likely to have tuberculosis. These high rates are almost entirely due to the unavailability of on-site medical attention.

In many small communities in the Arctic there is no hospital at all, and clinics are open only part-time—when physicians are able to visit. Doctors must find a way to get to these areas periodically to provide routine checkups and give vaccinations. Simply making the trip to the farflung Inuit communities and their more remote hunting camps is often the biggest challenge.

Many villages have no permanent roads into them from the outside because of the constant ice and snow. To reach these locations, doctors must travel by plane, helicopter, or boat. A special plane is used to fly emergencies to the nearest hospital. Large boats and planes with pontoons (large floats that are used to land the plane on the water) bring medical and other supplies to many Inuit communities near the water. These planes can also be outfitted with skis so they can take off from snow- or ice-covered land.

Many physicians today use the snowmobile, a small motorized sled on skis, to reach many remote Inuit outposts. Many, however, prefer to use the traditional dogsled, especially in the winter. A good team of dogs is often

Co-ops and the Arts

In the late 1950s the Inuit began to look for a way to produce income while at the same time maintaining their artistic traditions. By the end of the twentieth century nearly every native community had formed a cooperative—or co-op. This is a multipurpose operation that sells native works of art to faraway buyers. Many of them also manage hotels or fishing lodges or own taxi services and construction companies. All of the money made by these co-ops goes back into the business or community.

The talents of the Inuit are wide and varied. The Inupiat of northern Alaska, for instance, are known worldwide for their ivory carvings, while Inuit elsewhere are expert basket weavers. Baleen, the shiny, hard substance that comes from the whale's upper jaw, is used for making baskets in many parts of the Arctic.

The Tunooniq Theater is a successful group of Inuit actors in the Northwest Territories of Canada. Actors are able to write, produce, act in, and present very popular plays. One of their most popular plays is the Yunooniq Theater's *Changes*. It tells the story of Inuit life before, during, and after the coming of the white man.

The Inuit Broadcasting Corporation of Canada began producing Inuit shows in 1981. One cartoon show that is extremely popular with children features a character named Super Shamou, kind of an Inuit Superman.

Radio phone-in shows are also very popular in the Arctic. People call in when they want to sell something or when they just want to wish a friend happy birthday. Inuit hunters also announce over the local radio when they've made a kill and have meat to share with friends and families.

more reliable and certainly less expensive to use than a snowmobile. Unfortunately, even a top-notch racing dog team can average a speed of only twenty miles per hour. This is seldom sufficient for modern health care needs.

The Growing Problem of Pollution

In addition to the social and economic problems facing the Inuit today, they are also dealing with growing pollution in the Arctic. Industrial waste is the main threat to the Arctic at the present time. Air pollution from various companies has begun to poison many of the Inuit's traditional hunting grounds. Some Arctic scientists predict that polar bears will be as poisonous as toxic waste by the year 2005 if the level of pollutants continues to rise at the current rate.

Snowmobiles have benefited doctors and other Inuit in traveling across the Arctic tundra.

Furthermore, scientists agree that within twenty years the hunting of sea mammals will probably have to stop. This is not because of campaigns from animal rights activists, but rather due to the fact that by then the Arctic seas will be too polluted. Many whales and other marine animals are dying before their time, while newborns are not surviving into adulthood. As toxicologist Peter Ross states, "We [now] have the most contaminated marine mammals in the world."[46]

Another ongoing threat to the Arctic is the potential for deadly oil spills, such as the one that occurred off the Alaska coast in 1989. A few minutes after midnight on March 24, 1989, an oil tanker—the *Exxon Valdez*—struck a reef, causing the release of nearly eleven million gallons of oil into the surrounding waters. It was the largest oil spill in U.S. history. The oil polluted beaches and fishing waters for miles around and had a devastating impact on wildlife throughout the region.

Biologists and environmentalists continue their work to restore the balance of life as the twenty-first century begins. Most agree that the problem is very serious, and they are united in their belief that the Arctic must be saved. Today, international agreements are in force to protect many of the animals that live in the Arctic from hunting. Although most of the Arctic is still clean and wild, it will not stay that way for long if pollution-causing activities are not greatly modified. The Inuit are now working with scientists throughout the Arctic to monitor wildlife, but they have a long, uphill struggle ahead.

Life in the Arctic Today

Today there is a proud new feeling among the Inuit. Many of them are "going back to the land" by hunting and fishing again. They are relearning how to drive a dogsled, build a snow house, play Inuit games, and do the traditional dances. As an unidentified Inuit leader said, "It took fifty years to get to where we are now. We are confident we can . . . restore the dignity and self respect so many of our people have lost."[47]

Today's Inuit want to control their own lives as they did in the past. They work as teachers, radio announcers, police officers, and mechanics. Many are becoming doctors, lawyers, and engineers. Parents encourage their children to stay in school and go on to college. And in an effort to preserve Inuit culture, older people are coming to the schools and teaching the children all the old stories and legends.

Building homes in the Arctic today is very expensive due to the high cost of materials and transportation. The permafrost, which is made up of topsoil, rock, and ice, makes building very difficult. It stays permanently frozen to a depth of up to five thousand feet. Houses cannot be constructed directly on the ground because the heat inside the home could melt the permafrost. The foundations would then sink and the building would collapse. Therefore, most homes are built on stilts that are pounded into the frozen ground with a pile driver.

Homes in the Arctic also must be very well insulated. Some Inuit still build a tunnel

Hunting Today

The life of a hunter in today's Arctic is still hard and often dangerous. Modern life, however, has changed the methods and equipment used. High-powered rifles have replaced spears, while explosive metal harpoons are used instead of the traditional ones. Snowmobiles are ridden instead of dogsleds, and outboard motorboats have taken the place of kayaks and umiaks. Despite these advances, the Inuit still rely on their instincts to locate and kill the animals.

Today, hunters are faced with new problems. The Inuit face restrictions imposed by governmental and environmental groups on the animals they have always hunted. Although the Inuit were not the ones who hunted the whales to the edge of extinction, they are paying the price today by having to ask for special permission to hunt the whale.

Today, in many parts of the Arctic, school holidays are timed to coincide with spring hunting and summer fishing. And in a few Arctic communities the Inuit are returning to the old ways of hunting. Many villages have banned the use of snowmobiles because these noisy machines disrupt animal behavior patterns and make hunting difficult if not impossible. They have also banned the use of motorboats and have resumed hunting the bowhead whale from an umiak, using an old-fashioned harpoon. As it always has, hunting remains a vital and important part of Inuit culture.

Rifles have replaced spears as a method of hunting, though some Inuit are returning to traditional ways of hunting and fishing.

Many modern Inuit homes do not have flush toilets or a sewage system but do have the convenience of electricity.

of snow onto the entrance of their homes to serve as wind protectors. Most homes are made of wood and heated by an oil-burning stove. Snow houses are still used during hunting season and, in fact, many children to-day take "igloo building" as a lesson in school.

Some Standoffs with the Arctic—and Some Modern Improvements

Many Inuit homes don't have flush toilets be-cause there is no place for the sewage to go due to the frozen ground. Sewage in these houses is collected in strong bags and picked up by the famous "honey truck." These houses are also provided with water by a community truck that goes door-to-door. Other homes have a system of pipes to take away the sewage and another system to bring in water. These pipelines run above the ground or along shallow trenches and are well insulated to keep them from freezing.

Electricity is now available in most Inuit communities. Diesel generators produce the necessary power but are dependent on fuel, which can be delivered only in good weather. When a town's fuel supply runs out, the Inuit bring out their old oil lanterns and candles.

In many ways, Inuit communities look like those found in the United States and Canada. Modern schools and buildings line the streets. Libraries, athletic facilities, and theaters can be found in many of the larger towns. Grocery stores sell a wide variety of food, and clothing stores offer the latest fashions. Computers are used in schools for teaching many different subjects. Televisions and radios offer the latest news.

Despite these similarities, Inuit towns do have some pretty unique features. Many streets are filled not with cars, but with snow-mobiles and even dogsleds. People wear winter clothing all year round, so stores in the Arctic don't sell shorts or bathing suits. And instead of raccoons and dogs raiding garbage cans, a family in the Arctic might have to be on the lookout for polar bears. In fact, in Barrow, Alaska a few years ago, Halloween festivities had to be canceled because of the threat of polar bear attack!

Looking toward the Future

Many new and interesting economic programs are under way in Nunavut. Airlines,

The Messenger Feast

As darkness and frigid temperatures descended on the Arctic in 1988, more than two thousand Inupiat Inuit traveled to Barrow, Alaska, to take part in the Messenger Feast. This was the first time this celebration had been held in seventy years. Crammed into a tiny school gymnasium, the participants sang, danced, and exchanged gifts for three days.

The Messenger Feast was once the main social event for the Inuit in Alaska. It traditionally involved an exchange of gifts between a host village, which sponsored the event, and a guest village. The purpose was to enable people to trade goods and establish friendly relationships with other groups of Inuit.

In legend, the feast was "given" to the Inuit by the Sacred Eagle. It was named af-ter the messenger who traveled from village to village to deliver the invitations. In the early 1900s, however, missionaries banned the festival because it represented non-Christian beliefs.

Inuit leaders revived the celebration in the late 1980s in an effort to strengthen the old traditional ways of life. Messengers still participate but in only an honorary fashion since today the invitations go out by fax, e-mail, letter, or telephone. The spirit of sharing is the same as in the past as the Inuit open up their homes to out-of-town visitors. Banquets are prepared featuring traditional food while dancers from the various villages perform. Since 1988, attendance at the Messenger Feast has steadily increased.

offshore fisheries, ecotourism, hunting and fishing expeditions, and other businesses are helping to create many economic opportunities for the Inuit. Nunavut's economic future is also closely linked to its natural resources, mining, and oil development. This is true in Alaska and Greenland as well.

Most of today's Inuit follow a mixture of both Western (European and American) and traditional native practices. The attempt to balance the two ways of life are often confusing to the Inuit. According to a Canadian priest who lives with the Inuit, "The people tell me that they feel as if they are sitting between two chairs and can't find their place."[48]

Despite the many problems that still face the Inuit, they are a group of people who have learned to survive. The Inuit have endured a complete upheaval in the way of life that served them so well for three thousand years. However, the strength of their culture has premitted many traditions not only to survive but also to be rediscovered and adapted by Inuit living today.

As Canadian governor-general Romeo Le Blanc said at the celebration when Nunavut was created, "Through courage, sharing and ingenuity, the Inuit have prevailed in the harshest land on earth. You are the closest people on earth to the North Star. Tonight when Canadians look up at the North Star, we will remember your long history of courage, compassion and endurance."[49]

That statement is equally applicable to Inuit elsewhere. Their epic tale of survival in the Arctic is an inspirational one of courage, faith, and the ability to learn and adapt to a wild and punishing environment—and the modern world.

Notes

Introduction: Who Are the Inuit?

1. Philip Kopper, *The Smithsonian Book of North American Indians*. Washington, DC: Smithsonian Books, 1986, p. 95.
2. Quoted in Tapirisat of Canada, "The History of the Inuit." www.tapirisat.ca.
3. Quoted in Tapirisat of Canada, "The History of the Inuit."

Chapter 1: Surviving in a Harsh Land

4. Quoted in National Geographic, *Canada's Incredible Coasts*. Washington, DC: National Geographic Books, 1991, p. 130.
5. Paula Younkin, *Indians of the Arctic and Subarctic*. New York: Facts on File, 1992, p. 7.
6. Quoted in Time-Life, *The American Indians: People of the Ice and Snow*. Alexandria, VA: Time-Life Books, 1994, p. 90.
7. George E. Stuart, *Ancient Pioneers: The First Americans*. Washington, D.C.: National Geographic Books, 2001, p. 43.

Chapter 2: Hunters of the Far North

8. Jason Gardner, *The Sacred Earth*. Novato, CA: New World Library, 1998, p. xix.
9. Barry Lopez, *Of Wolves and Men*. New York: Touchstone, 1978, p. 91.

10. Stuart, *Ancient Pioneers,* p. 47.
11. Stuart, *Ancient Pioneers,* p. 27.
12. Quoted in Time-Life, *The American Indians: People of the Ice and Snow,* p. 73.
13. Quoted in Time-Life, *The American Indians: People of the Ice and Snow,* p. 81.
14. Quoted in Reader's Digest, *America's Fascinating Indian Heritage*. Pleasantville, NY: Reader's Digest Association, 1978, p. 361.
15. Quoted in Alaska Northwest Book, *The Alaska Almanac*. Anchorage, AK: Northwest Books, 1998, p. 148.

Chapter 3: Family and Community

16. Quoted in Time-Life, *The American Indians: People of the Ice and Snow,* p. 100.
17. Younkin, *Indians of the Arctic and Subarctic,* p. 10.
18. Ron Fisher, *America: AD 1000*. Washington, DC: National Geographic Books, 1999, p. 40.
19. Quoted in *Canada and the World Backgrounder,* "Nunavut: Social Conditions," March 1999.
20. Younkin, *Indians of the Arctic and Subarctic,* p. 64.

Chapter 4: Religion and Ritual

21. Quoted in Time-Life, *The American Indians: The Spirit World.* Alexandria, VA: Time-Life Books, 1992, p. 14.
22. Younkin, *Indians of the Arctic and Subarctic,* p. 63.
23. Time-Life Editors, *The American Indians: People of the Ice and Snow,* p. 122.
24. Joseph Campbell, *Primitive Mythology: The Mask of God.* New York: Penguin Books, 1959, p. 243.
25. Campbell, *Primitive Mythology,* p. 243.
26. Campbell, *Primitive Mythology,* p. 244.
27. Campbell, *Primitive Mythology,* p. 244.
28. Quoted in Time-Life, *The American Indians: The Spirit World,* p. 70.
29. Quoted in Time-Life, *The American Indians: The Spirit World,* p. 68.

Chapter 5: The Coming of the White Man

30. Quoted in Time-Life, *The American Indians: People of the Ice and Snow,* p. 142.
31. Quoted in Time-Life, *The American Indians: People of the Ice and Snow,* p. 147.
32. Tapirisat of Canada, "Our 5000 Year History." www.tapirisat.ca, p. 10.
33. Barry Lopez, *Arctic Dreams.* New York: Bantam Publications, 1986, p. 6.
34. Younkin, *Indians of the Arctic and Subarctic,* p. 83.
35. Quoted in Tapirisat of Canada, "Our 5000 Year History."
36. Quoted in Younkin, *Indians of the Arctic and Subarctic,* p. 83.
37. Quoted in Time-Life, *The American Indians: People of the Ice and Snow,* p. 174.
38. John Geddes, "Canada: Northern Dawn," *MacLeans,* February 1999.
39. Encyclopedia Britannica Editors, "The Inuit," *Encyclopedia Britannica.* www.britannica.com.

Chapter 6: Entering the Twenty-first Century

40. Habeeb Salloum, "Nunavut: Canada's Newest Child," *Contemporary Review,* August 1999.
41. Quoted in Salloum, "Nunavut."
42. Michael Parfit, "A Dream Called Nunavut," *National Geographic,* September 1997, p. 74.
43. Quoted in Salloum, "Nunavut."
44. *Canada and the World Backgrounder,* "Nunavut: Social Conditions."
45. Quoted in Geddes, "Canada."
46. Quoted in Marguerite Holloway, "Sea Sick," *Discover,* February 2001, p. 51.
47. Quoted in Salloum, "Nunavut."
48. Quoted in National Geographic, *Canada's Incredible Coasts,* p. 132.
49. Quoted in Salloum, "Nunavut."

For Further Reading

Bryan and Cherry Alexander, *Inuit.* Austin, TX: Raintree, Steck and Vaughn, 1993. An excellent book about the Inuit today. The authors have written extensively about the Inuit and their way of life.

————, *What Do We Know about the Inuit?* New York: Peter Bedrick Books, 1995. This book answers specific questions about the Inuit, their culture, their religion, and their future.

Ian Barrett, *Tundra and People.* Morristown, NJ: Silver Burdett, 1982. A book about the Far North, its landscape, and its people.

Beyond the High Hills: A Book of Eskimo Poems. Cleveland: World Publishing, 1961. This book is what the title suggests, a book of Eskimo poems for children.

Mary Bringle, *Eskimos.* New York: Franklin Watts, 1973. An older work for children, looking at the Eskimos' way of life.

Hugh Brody, *Living Arctic: Hunters of the Canadian North.* Seattle: University of Washington Press, 1990. A scholarly study of the Inuit and their traditional way of life.

Fred Bruemmer, *Arctic Memories: Living with the Inuit.* Toronto: Key Porter, 1995. The author writes of his experiences living with the Inuit.

Adam Bryant, *Canada.* Parsippany, NJ: Dillon Press, 1997. A good book about the peoples and culture of Canada, including some information about the Inuit.

Monica Byles, *Life in the Polar Lands.* New York: Franklin Watts, 1990. A book about life in the polar regions, including wildlife, plants, and people.

Theodore A. Rees Cheney, *Living in Polar Regions.* New York: Franklin Watts, 1987. A children's book about life in the Arctic and Antarctic.

Jennifer Fleischner, *The Inuit: People of the Arctic.* Brookfield, CT: Millbrook Press, 1995. This is an excellent book about the Inuit, their culture, and their way of life.

Peter Freuchen, *Book of Eskimos.* New York: Fawcett World Library, 1961. An older book about the Eskimos.

Lyn Hancock, *Discover Canada: Northwest Territories.* Toronto: Grolier Limited, 1993. An excellent look at the Northwest Territories in Canada, home to thousands of Inuit.

Andrew Haslem and Alexandra Parsons, *Arctic Peoples.* New York: Thomson Learning, 1995. A book about the various native peoples who live in the Arctic.

Wally Herbert, *Eskimos.* New York: Franklin Watts, 1977. A children's book about the Eskimos.

Diane Hoyt-Goldsmith, *Arctic Hunter.* New York: Holiday House, 1992. A book about a young Inuit man in modern society and the hunting that his family still does.

Jill Hughes, *Eskimos.* New York: Gloucester Press, 1978. An older book that still has some excellent information about the Inuit and their traditional way of life.

Bobbie Kalman, *The Arctic Land.* New York: Crabtree Publishing, 1988. An excellent book about the area of the world called the Arctic.

Bobbie Kalman and William Belsey, *An Arctic Community.* New York: Crabtree, 1988. An excellent look at life today in one Inuit community.

J. C. H. King, *First Peoples, First Contacts.* Cambridge, MA: Harvard University Press, 1999. This book has an excellent chapter on the peoples of the Arctic.

Shirlee P. Newman, *The Inuit.* New York: Franklin Watts, 1993. This is an excellent book on the Inuit from past to present.

Kevin Osborn, *The Peoples of the Arctic.* New York: Chelsea House, 1990. A children's book about the various peoples and cultures of the Arctic.

David Rootes, *The Arctic.* Minneapolis: Lerner, 1996. A book about the Arctic and the people who live there.

Donna Walsh Shepherd. *Alaska,* New York: Childrens Press, 1999. A good look at the State of Alaska, including some information about the Inuit.

Works Consulted

Books

Alaska Northwest Books, *The Alaska Almanac*. Anchorage, AK: Northwest Books, 1998. A book filled with facts about Alaska, including some information about the Inuit.

Joseph Campbell, *Primitive Mythology: The Mask of God*. New York: Penguin Books, 1959. There is a small section in this book on Inuit shamanism and religious life.

Ron Fisher, *America: AD 1000*. Washington, DC: National Geographic Books, 1999. There is an excellent chapter in this book on the peoples of the Arctic around the year 1000, including good information about the Thule Culture, ancestors of the present-day Inuit.

Jason Gardner, *The Sacred Earth*. Novato, CA: New World Library, 1998. A group of quotes and stories about the earth from naturalists and writers.

Elizabeth Hahn, *The Inuit*. Vero Beach, FL: Rourke, 1990. An excellent book about the Inuit and their way of life.

Joan Halifax, *Shamanic Voices*. New York: E. P. Dutton, 1979. An adult book about shamanic cultures around the world. There are several offerings from the Inuit.

Philip Kopper, *The Smithsonian Book of North American Indians*. Washington, D.C.: Smithsonian Books, 1986. A general book dealing with many native peoples, done by region and covering the land and the culture.

Gilbert Legay, *Atlas of Indians*. Hauppauge, NY: Barrons Educational Series, 1993. A book that looks at Native Americans by region.

Barry Lopez, *Arctic Dreams*. New York: Bantam, 1986. This book offers excellent insights and information about the Inuit from an author who spent much time in the Arctic, living in a number of different Inuit villages.

————, *Of Wolves and Men*. New York: Touchstone, 1978. A classic book about the wolf and its interactions with humankind throughout the ages. An excellent section on what the animal has taught humankind about hunting.

Robert McGee, *Historical Atlas of Canada*. Toronto: University of Toronto Press, 1987. A general look at Canadian history with a good section on the Inuit.

Lawrence Millman, *A Kayak Full of Ghosts: Eskimo Tales*. Santa Barbara, CA: Capra, 1987. A wonderful book chock-full of Eskimo tales, stories, and myths. Some are violent and graphic.

David Murdock, *North American Indians*. New York: Alfred A. Knopf, 1995. This is an Eyewitness Book with excellent illustrations, covering many Native American groups, including the Inuit.

National Geographic, *Canada's Incredible Coasts*. Washington, DC: National Geographic Books, 1991. There is an excellent chapter in this book on the Inuits, called "Icy Reaches of the North."

Reader's Digest, *America's Fascinating Indian Heritage*. Pleasantville, NY: Reader's Digest Association, 1978. An excellent book about various Native American groups done by region. There is a lengthy and very informative section on the Inuit.

David Rootes, *Exploration into the Polar Regions*. New York: New Discovery, 1994. A book that looks at the exploration of both the Arctic and Antarctic throughout the ages.

Donald M. Silver, *Arctic Tundra*. New York: W. H. Freeman, 1994. An exciting journey through the Arctic tundra.

George E. Stuart, *Ancient Pioneers: The First Americans*. Washington, DC: National Geographic Books, 2001. This book takes a look at many different Native American groups before the coming of the white man, including an excellent section about the Inuit.

Barbara Taylor, *Arctic and Antarctic*. New York: Alfred A. Knopf, 1995. This book takes a general look at the regions of the Arctic and Antarctic, focusing on the people, climate, and wildlife.

Time-Life, *The American Indians: Cycles of Life*. Alexandria, VA: Time-Life Books, 1994. This book is one of a series and gives an overall look at Native Americans and their different rites of passage.

————, *The American Indians: People of the Ice and Snow.* Alexandria, VA: Time-Life Books, 1994. This book contains wonderful information and numerous pictures related to the Inuit. Excellent reference.

————, *The American Indians: The Spirit World.* Alexandria, VA: Time-Life Books, 1992. This book is one of a series on the Indians of North America. This particular volume deals with religious life and the rituals of many different groups, including the Inuit.

Paula Younkin, Indians of the Arctic and Subarctic. New York: Facts on File, 1992. A book about the different peoples who live in the Far North. There is some excellent information on the Inuit and their way of life.

Magazines and Journals

Associated Press, "Inuits Seek to Hunt a Bowhead," March 20, 2000. A brief article about a request by the Inuit to hunt a bowhead whale as part of their hunting tradition.

Ann Blackman and John F. Dickerson, "War Over Arctic Oil," *Time,* February 19, 2001. This article describes the conflict between Alaskan natives and the Unitedf States government over further oil and gas drilling in Alaska.

Canada and the World Backgrounder, "Nunavut: Government," March 1999. This article and the three that follow are part of an intensive look at Nunavut and the Inuits of Canada.

————, "Nunavut: Land Claim," March 1999.

————, "Nunavut: Social Conditions," March 1999.

————, "Nunavut: The Past," March 1999.

Milton M. R. Freeman, "Native People: Arctic," *The 1998 Canadian Encyclopedia,* September 1997. This article gives an overview of the various indigenous peoples of the Arctic.

John Geddes, "Canada: Northern Dawn," *MacLeans,* February 1999. This article talks about Nunavut, the new Canadian territory of the Inuit.

Marguerite Holloway, "Sea Sick," *Discover,* February 2001. An excellent article about the growing pollution of the oceans and how it is affecting marine wildlife.

Len Jenshel and Diane Cook, "Greenland," *National Geographic Traveler,* July/August 2000. A short article about one northwest Greenland town.

Dane Lanken and Mary Vincent, "Nunavut Up and Running," *Canadian Geographic,* January 1999. A discussion of Nunavut and some of the issues that face the Inuit.

Thomas A. Lewis, "High Stakes in a Land of Plenty," *National Wildlife,* June/July 1987. An article looking at the controversial issue of drilling for oil in the Arctic National Wildlife Refuge in Alaska, which could have potentially devastating effects on the caribou herds.

JoAnn Lowell, "Rebirthing Traditions," *Contemporary Women's Issues Database,* March 1995. An article about returning to more traditional ways of childbirth for the Inuit.

Jenny Manzer, "Inuit Health Care Needs Get Lost in the Shuffle," *Medical Post,* March 2000. A look at many of the health problems of the Inuits.

Reed McManus, "Where the Caribou Roam," *Sierra,* July/August,2000. An article that focuses on the danger to the Porcupine Caribou Herd in Alaska, which is to be affected by American legislation in the near future.

Michael Parfit, "A Dream Called Nunavut," *National Geographic*, September 1997. This article looks at the new Canadian territory called Nunavut.

Habeeb Salloum, "Nunavut: Canada's Newest Child," *Contemporary Review,* August 1999. The author talks with one of the leaders of the Nunavut movement.

Ed Struzik, "Journey to Nunavut," *International Wildlife,* March 1999. The author takes a trip with one of the leaders of the Inuit movement toward independence.

Internet Sources

Encyclopedia Britannica Editors, "The Inuit," Encyclopedia Britannica. www.britannica.com.

Tapirisat of Canada, "The History of the Inuit." www.tapirisat.ca.

Tapirisat of Canada, "Our 5000 Year History." www.tapirisat.ca.

Websites

Arctic Culture. www.arcticculture.about.com. This website features some wonderful information about the Arctic and the people who live there.

Inupiat Inuit of Alaska. www.ankn.uaf.edu/inupiaq.html. This website deals exclusively with the Inuit.

Phil Konstatin, Eskimo Words. www.urbanlegends.com. This website includes a dictionary of Inuit words.

Nunavut. www.nunavut.com. This website is devoted to a study of the Inuit and the area of Canada known as Nunavut.

Polar Net. www.polarnet.ca/polarnet/nunavut.htm. This website discusses the new government of Nunavut and the Inuit.

Tapirisat of Canada. www.tapirisat.ca. This is an excellent website containing a great deal of information about the Inuit of Canada and Nunavut.

"Writing in Inuktitut." www.halfmoon.org. This website offers a glimpse at the Inuktitut alphabet.

Index

Picture Credits

Cover photo: © Clark Mishler/Alaska Stock Images/PictureQuest

© AFP/CORBIS, 25

© Shaun Best/Reuters, 84

© Bettmann/CORBIS, 80

Digital Stock, 18, 33, 37

© Peter Harholdt/CORBIS, 54, 66, 73

© Hulton/Archive by Getty Images, 20, 36, 44, 46, 70

© Wolfgang Kaehler/CORBIS, 69

© Alain Le Garsmeur/CORBIS, 91

Library of Congress, 19, 22, 23, 24, 32, 38, 41, 47, 48, 50, 52, 71, 77

© Michael Maslan Historic Photographs/CORBIS, 60, 63, 75

Brandy Noon, 12

© North Wind Pictures, 72

© Pat O'Hara/CORBIS, 90

© Galen Rowell/CORBIS, 30

© Paul A. Souders/CORBIS, 53

© Hubert Stadler/CORBIS, 65

© Roger Tidman/CORBIS, 88

Werner Forman Archive/British Museum, London/Art Resource, NY, 58

Werner Forman Archive/Eskimo Museum, Churchill, Canada/Art Resource, NY, 11

Werner Forman Archive/National Museum, Denmark/Art Resource, NY, 59, 61

Werner Forman Archive/National Museum of Man, Ottawa/Art Resource, NY, 10

© K. M. Westermann/CORBIS, 40

© Staffan Widstrand/CORBIS, 15, 17, 34

© Doug Wilson/CORBIS, 82

About the Author

Anne Wallace Sharp is the author of one adult book, *Gifts,* a compilation of hospice stories, and one other children's book, *Daring Women Pirates.* In addition, she has written numerous magazine articles for both the adult and children's markets. A retired registered nurse, she also has a degree in history. Her interests include writing, reading, traveling, and spending time with her grandchildren. Anne lives in Beavercreek, Ohio.